Cameroon's Contemporary Culture and Politics:
Prospects and Problems

Milton Krieger

Langaa Research & Publishing CIG
Mankon, Bamenda

Publisher

Langaa RPCIG

Langaa Research & Publishing Common Initiative Group
P.O. Box 902 Mankon
Bamenda
North West Region
Cameroon
Langaagrp@gmail.com
www.langaa-rpcig.net

Distributed in and outside N. America by African Books Collective
orders@africanbookscollective.com
www.africanbookcollective.com

ISBN: 9956-790-27-3

For permissions to reproduce original texts for this volume, the publisher and author thank the following:

Boston University African Studies Center for "Language in Cameroon, 1960-1990: Bilingual Policy, Multilingual Practice." Issues in Language and Education Series, 1991.

Indiana University Press for "Building the Republic through Letters: Abbia: Cameroon Cultural Review, 1963-82, and Its Legacy," Research in African Literatures 27, 2 (1996), pp. 155-177, and "In Memoriam: Thomas Melone," Research in African Literatures 29, 1 (1998), pp. 197-199 (ISSN 0034-5210).

Cambridge University Press for "Cameroon's Democratic Crossroads, 1990-4," The Journal of Modern African Studies 32, 4 (1994), pp. 605-628 (ISSN 0022-278X).

About the cover

The book's cover reproduces that of *Abbia*, Cameroon's remarkable journal of culture, 1963-1982. Its text seeks to emulate *Abbia*'s broad coverage and high standards.

Table of Contents

Acknowledgments

Many professional and personal debts have accrued during the quarter century I've studied Cameroon. Citations in four texts published 1991-1998, now reprinted here, and in two books published later, record my gratitude to those who've contributed along the way.

For this, my final Cameroon scholarly work, added thanks are due. Richard Bjornson and Victor Le Vine paved my way to Cameroon studies either side of 1990; Richard's sudden death in 1992 deprived me and others of his advice and enthusiasm but Victor's generosity continued until his death in 2010. Paul Nchoji Nkwi, then responsible for research protocols at the ministry of higher education and research, facilitated my own and my wife's first visit in 1989 and remained our guide for a decade. Dr. Philip and Cecelia Noss welcomed us and many other "expats" in Yaounde, using their years of Cameroon experience and expertise to impart knowledge and provide hospitality. The late Augustine Tih was John Ngu Foncha's driver either side of 1960; he, his family and compound graciously hosted and sustained us in Bamenda through the 1990s. Ni John Fru Ndi generously opened doors to the latter parts of this book, and many more thereafter Two other Cameroonians stand out among my friends and scholarly advisors since 1995, continuing past my last time there in 1999 to the present, Alhaji Sariki Umaru and Sarli Sardou Nana; it is a sad measure of the country's condition that they are now abroad, where their experiences and skills are deployed more than at home. Francis Nyamnjoh's energies and talents have kept my *in absentia* focus on Cameroon since we met in 1999, while he traverses Africa and beyond as a teacher and scholar, and develops Langaa into the unique venture I am glad and proud to be part of; we collaborated nursing this text to print. Western Washington University continues to fund my

Cameroon scholarship a decade since my retirement, including the valuable work of two Liberal Studies department student assistants, Eliah Drake-Raue and especially Clarissa Mansfield.

This book is dedicated to my wife Judy. She spent fifteen years giving our family and my career her priority and their shape, resumed studies step-by-step, stayed sturdy, and at the time we reached Cameroon was very nearly the oldest woman from the U.S.A. ever to initiate anthropology field research for the Ph.D. in tropical Africa. She completed it successfully and then developed her own academic career, though it was constrained by time and circumstance. Her fellowships for Cameroon study funded more of our time there than I did, her research path and resilience enriched my experience during and beyond the decade of our travels there, and her myriad skills and interests continue to do so. For these and many other reasons, this one's for Ma Ju, with love and admiration.

Prologue

Scholarly background and research bearings

A quarter century separates my first step on Cameroonian soil in 1989 and this reprint of my short writings from the 1990s, with my retrospective commentary on them. In its broadest terms, the book charts a decade's cross-section of the country's erratic recent course, which subordinates a capable citizenry's aspirations and an ample resource base to a statecraft marginalizing or victimizing many Cameroonians. It turns some of the finest away from public into private pursuits, causes others to leave by choice or under duress, to the nation's far higher costs than benefits, and claims casualties and fatalities.

Both my own story and the country's frame this volume, I hope not to the latter's detriment. Cameroon entered my scholarly life, and so much more as friendships developed, past mid-career. Trained primarily in medieval English constitutional history through a University of Toronto doctorate completed in 1969, I had by then already taught four years in the pre-modern European parts of an undergraduate history department and humanities program curriculum. But, just past the age of thirty and in the academic community's 1960s youth cohort, I was restless. Involved in campus Vietnam War protest, the vexing question "where does my future lie?" fitted the times. In professional particulars, would a 15th century focus hold my scholarly interest going forward? While a favorable seller's market for North American scholars remained in place (though not for long) and with a Ph.D and a teaching apprenticeship in hand, an alternative, more engaging field looked appealing, and possible.

Africa was the prime candidate. Curiosity began when my family hosted a Nigerian fencer at the 1954 Empire and Commonwealth Games in Vancouver. South Africa leading up to and past

Sharpeville, 1960, sparked my earliest political movement interest. As a change of pace in 1968, I taught a seminar "South Africa in Revolution," a fitting if slightly premature title for that globally explosive year. Both I and my students found its issues and materials more compelling than my standard survey courses and seminars on "Chaucer's England," "Oliver Cromwell and the English Revolution" and "The Age of Louis XIV."

A fresh start in 1970 with another undergraduate program, Western Washington University's Liberal Studies department, let me combine familiar Western Civilization teaching (until 1990) with a new, gradually acquired teaching and then research competence on Africa. Three months each at the University of Wisconsin and in Kaduna and Nairobi, 1975-1976, provided my first African academic and field experiences. Edris Makward in literature and Robert Koehl and Robert Tabachnick in education policy at Wisconsin, then Okot p'Bitek and Ngugi wa Thiong'o in Nairobi, were that time's important mentors along my new academic path. Brief 1976-1985 encounters beyond their writings with Camara Laye, Chinua Achebe and Wole Soyinka enlarged my sense of Africans at the frontiers and on the barricades where great literature, political confrontations and panoramic critiques of culture and the public realm converge.

Guided also by the Renaissance civic humanism that transformed the medieval European world's experience and imagination I'd previously studied and taught, transferring that inquiry to contemporary Africa and factoring in the parallel 20th century challenges to established authority structures, I formulated a number of questions. How are culture, education and language policies in independent African states directed, if at all, to contemporary priorities and values? What visions of national development and community direct them? And how successful, or not, are these efforts likely to be as Africans, with sovereign statehood largely secured, seek to reclaim (beyond the political formalities) their own historical bearings and to create an autonomous future of their own choosing?

My first substantial African research and writing, undertaken in 1985 at (its name then) the University of Ife and published in 1987, applied these questions to the Western Region of Nigeria's minister of education in the mid-1950s, Stephen Awokoya. Robert July's *An African Voice: the role of the humanities in African independence* also appeared in 1987 and provided a fully synoptic framework for my approach to African Studies. To investigate, evaluate and integrate the study of contemporary Africa's culture, education and language policies, in practice and as ideal, became my settled project, directed to "whither Africa?" questions of long term national and continental development.

Expecting to continue research in Nigeria by branching out from the Awokoya study, deteriorating conditions there and my wife's doctoral field work in anthropology took us instead to Cameroon in 1989. My Canadian background and many courses in French through my first university degree made Cameroon, with its official French-English bilingualism, reflecting Canada's in reverse ratios, a manageable research site with clearly promising prospects. Richard Bjornson, along the way to his 1991 book *The African Quest for Freedom and Identity: Cameroonian Writing and the National Experience*, directed the specific application of my own and July's work to Cameroon and generously provided research contacts. Jean-François Bayart's, Richard Joseph's, Victor Le Vine's and others' scholarship, directed in various ways to the nature of the African state and its Cameroon setting, which made the country so prominent for the study of Africa, 1960-1990, addressed my apprenticeship's starkest needs.

I first arrived there 24 January 1989, prepared to engage Cameroon and Cameroonians wherever the search for convergence between humanistic efforts and contemporary public life might take me. Thus began a "Cameroon decade" with four research visits that gave me over two years on the ground, 1989-1999. It generated the writings reproduced in this volume, followed by a co-authored 1998 book with Joseph Takougang on Cameroon's political history, 1960-1997, and another of my own on the Social Democratic Front (hereafter SDF) in 2008.

ix

The texts reproduced below are presented in their original form, except for editing where original errors or inconsistencies in diction and punctuation may have misled earlier readers, and could also do so for this later audience. I offer both those 1990s contributions to Cameroon scholarship and my reflections on them as of 2013, for better where I approximated the truth, for worse where I did not; faults are, as always, my own.

Chapter 1

Language and education: fault lines appear

Everyone reading this book will understand Cameroon's experience as of 1989, but a brief account of its emergence as a nation state remains in order, to prepare what follows. Colonized first by Germany for thirty years until World War I, when known as Kamerun, its conquest and divided transfer, first to French and British League of Nations mandate and then to United Nations trust territory status, prevailed until independence and a (still contested) reunification in 1960-1961. A roughly three-quarter French to (bordering Nigeria) one-quarter British ratio in matters like formal governance, population and my specific "legacy" research concerns, culture, education and language, continued in effect past 1961 in a federal republic's francophone East Cameroun and anglophone West Cameroon. But two francophone presidents engineered constitutional changes against the federation grain. Ahmadou Ahidjo's 1972 referendum established a "United Republic" with reduced anglophone autonomy and Paul Biya's decree in 1984 dropped any qualifier and created what many dissident anglophones, believing their rights and protections to have been breached and dissolved, came bitterly to term (reverting to the pre-reunification title) "la république du Cameroun." Political dynamics, of course, generated the constitutional changes. An increasingly monolithic state emerged as the response to a determined opposition's long struggle led by the Union of Cameroon Peoples political party, formed after World War II and spread from French into British late colonial terrains and through the first decade of Ahidjo's presidency, which was challenged as neo-colonialist. He assembled the ruling Cameroon National Union party as the state's political agency during and past federation times. Biya, in the wake of a mutinous 1984 backlash by northerners against his 1982 succession to Ahidjo, reorganized his

1

party inheritance as the Cameroon Peoples Democratic Movement (hereafter CPDM) in 1985.

Such were the formal trappings of the politics and public life I encountered on arrival in 1989. Reading veteran Cameroonian scholars and writers like Jean-Marc Ela and René Philombe and the next generation's talents like Achille Mbembe, and meeting informants like Kenjo Jumbam, Patrick Mbunwe Samba, Jean Mfoulou, Ba'bila Mutia and Omer Yembe, revealed the contested aftermath of the reconstruction of state and party. The recent decline in economic performance was clear from statistical data and from anecdotes like 1989's beer replacing 1979's champagne among elites, with palm wine for beer the commoners' parallel. Cameroon was less unified and more contentious than the serene experience and bright prospects projected in Biya's iconography on public display, including the front page of the government's daily *Cameroon Tribune* newspaper, and in the 1987 book published under his name, *Pour le liberalisme communautaire* (Engl., *Communal Liberalism*). Hugh MacLennan's 1945 novel *Two Solitudes*, the classic English language literary expression of Canada's English-French tensions, and Jacques Benjamin's *Les camerounaises occidentaux: la minorité dans un état bicommunautaire* (1972), a French-Canadian's analysis in the wake of 1970's separation crisis in Québec, alerted me to Cameroon parallels in 1989. It took little time to recognize problematic affinities between Cameroon's condition and what I recognized growing up in Canada and as still a factor, with opposite population, culture and language ratios. They became clear, through research, experience and anecdote during my shuttle for seven months in 1989, principally between francophone Yaounde and the city and rural hinterland of Bamenda, capital of North West (then) Province and one of anglophone Cameroonians' two major population hubs.

A document found early in my research, an "Open Letter To All English-Speaking Parents of Cameroon from the English speaking students of the North West and South West Provinces" (i.e., those with most to lose in the future) stood out. It first appeared 20 August 1985, five months after the founding congress of the ruling CPDM held in Bamenda, circulating only in mimeograph form. This "New Deal Congress" had been designed both to inaugurate Biya's own party and to convince minority anglophones that they were secure from assimilation. But the eight page Open Letter's rejoinder presented a bill of particulars and attacked the entire range of state initiatives since 1960-1961, including the hypocrisy its authors found in the Bamenda proceedings. As quoted in the first of my writings reprinted below, and perhaps its central challenge: "Tell us why bilingualism...demands the mastery of the French language by Anglophones and not vice versa."

The second indication of tension, more public than 1985's Open Letter, was the ministry of education's Etats-Généraux in April 1989, an official, plenary policy forum. Refused access as an observer, I trolled press accounts and interviewed six participants about the proceedings after their conclusion. Summoned to debate and recommend policy for the ministry, the session broke up when the minister, Georges Ngango, known as a CPDM "reformer" at its 1985 Bamenda Congress, was (literally) tapped on the shoulder at the podium and led from the hall as his removal from cabinet was announced on the mid-day national radio news. Whether he was the instigator or the victim of the crisis, Ngango's fate was sealed by fierce debate in the hall over the issue of "harmonization," the euphemism for tighter realignment of all state schools to the francophone model. How sensitive was the debate? To quote my 1991 text again: "the police and army were placed on alert against public demonstrations in the two anglophone provinces, and school principals were dispatched back from Yaounde to keep the peace on those campuses with student bodies old enough to breach it."

Whereas the Open Letter's original appearance was furtive, the Etats-Généraux played out quite publicly during my first 1989 weeks in Cameroon. These two shards of experience established my bearings and set my compass for the 1991 paper and all that followed. They influenced (beyond pure scholarship's prompts) my research and contacts as they developed, and revealed Cameroon's complexities and rivalries I'd need to factor into my study of its culture-education-language-development matrix.

Research in Nigeria for the Awokoya paper had already acquainted me with the Six-Year Primary School Project there, which used the Yoruba language as a medium of instruction in the Western Region's early schooling. Adding to that experience, I became familiar in the course of 1989 with the cognate socio- and applied linguistics work already published or still in preparation and kindly shared with me by Maurice Tadadjeu, previously generated and now fully activated on his way through Georgetown University and University of Southern California post-graduate degrees to his academic post and his research and agency work on and off the University of Yaounde campus since 1977. This scholarly background and my experience in Yaounde's and Bamenda's streets and elsewhere reinforced my sense that language(s) in Cameroon raised interesting, even abiding practical, policy and political issues, with applications throughout my fields of enquiry.

From these origins came two research projects developed in 1989. The first of them unfolds in what remains of Chapter 1, with language(s) as a facet of national development policy its focus. The second is Chapter 2's centerpiece, with the journal *Abbia* its focus. But it should be made clear here that these two items, published in 1991 and 1996 and reprinted in the present volume, drew on mutually reinforcing research and writing started in 1989, and can be read as two variations on my generic, simultaneous, overlapping studies of culture, education, language and development.

Tadadjeu (a francophone) and his two colleagues in the university's department of African Languages and Linguistics, its head Emmanuel Chia and Sammy Beban Chumbow (anglophones; the collaboration across their varied original and European languages was notable), provided current materials and the access and leads to people I consulted during my seven month 1989 Cameroon residency as the first project emerged. Tadadjeu's scholarly prominence registered when he was chosen to deliver the keynote address to the April 1989 forum that ended with Ngango's dismissal from cabinet.

4

His role in that forum, and its abrupt end, further alerted me to the public and controversial dimensions of my topic.

Yaounde at large, not just the university campus, was this first paper's primary research venue. I found a rather scant and patchy run of materials from ministry sources for statistics and planning documents but also (in compensation) a far more productive network of connections and publications through Tadadjeu and his colleagues. Their applied linguistics efforts, spanning indigenous and exogenous languages, had created PROPELCA (Projet de Recherche Opérationelle pour l'Enseignement des Langues au Cameroun). It was being fielded in primary schools with support from a key external agency with, by 1989, a substantial research and residential site in Yaounde and roughly two dozen branch operations deployed in a majority of Cameroon's ten provinces, Société Internationale de Linguistique (originally known in its U.S.A. base as Wycliffe Bible Translators and then as Summer Institute of Linguistics; there is a history of controversy over its religious advocacy and allegations of ties to U.S.A. covert operations in Latin America, but these issues have never to my knowledge become a matter of private concern or public debate in Cameroon).

A complex set of objectives and activities drove PROPELCA and SIL as they approached Cameroon's 250+ indigenous languages within the global framework of 6,000-7,000 languages likely to decline or disappear before achieving written form or, even if written, to be displaced by larger languages. Tadadjeu used the term "trilingualisme extensif" to cover the transactional dynamics between Cameroon's two European official languages and any specific mother tongue as parts of research and projects developed locally and phased into schools at appropriate curricular points. PROPELCA emphasized experimental pedagogy and addressed practical issues of Cameroonians' effective language acquisition for a variety of purposes in the broad arena of national development that interested me. Its domain included both the "language of instruction" protocols of the Yoruba project I'd recently studied and indigenous language "content" features. SIL's primary purpose, in keeping with its

5

evangelical Protestant calling, was the creation of New Testament texts in local languages not yet in written form. But it also produced indigenous language training manuals and small scale, familiar "daily life" publications, with content ranging from customary stories to crafts and livelihoods, for enjoyment and for basic needs edification and guidance, meant to introduce and advance SIL's larger design via quotidian written indigenous language productions. These PROPELCA and SIL initiatives, singly or jointly, also organized language committees of local notables to inscribe and valorize twenty-three previously unwritten languages by 1989, with Bafut, Mundani and other projects on anglophone terrain and their counterparts in francophone Cameroon, from south to north.

PROPELCA's and SIL's diverse initiatives were broadly compatible and mutually supportive in their work on language repertoire development, engaging and juggling Cameroon's indigenous and exogenous languages in varied ways. As a national enterprise, PROPELCA had nominal encouragement though not much fiscal or logistic support from ministries, but the University of Yaounde was a stable academic base. SIL brought people from North America and Europe and trained Cameroonians for its work. Its enterprise, financed by both its own office and communities of faith overseas, was committed to long term linguistic field work and was staged at a computerized operational facility just south of Yaounde's urban core that serviced its field projects.

Such were the genesis and framework for my own scholarship, sketched and researched in Cameroon during 1989, written up in 1990 after I returned home, published in 1991 as a Boston University monograph "Language in Cameroon, 1960-1990: Bilingual Policy, Multilingual Practice" and now reproduced here. Its policy background was sketched largely by reference to its driving force, Bernard Nsokika Fonlon (covered more thoroughly in Chapter 2 below). Its practice foreground was mainly Tadadjeu's PROPELCA-SIL domain.

The original version carried no abstract. But a retrospective abstract if written in 2013 would cite 1) my effort to chart the

6

promotion and emergence of Cameroon's indigenous languages in written form, as new and potentially effective vehicles alongside the two official European languages for national development purposes, and 2) my sense that the effort encountered, and was limited by, delicate balances of interest and the need to manage and maintain national unity within a highly pluralistic and (it became clear) contested public life and political culture. From the two flashpoints already noted, 1985's Open Letter and 1989's Etats-Généraux, and what I surmised from the modest official backing for PROPELCA, came my pervasive sense of measured caution, not experimental risk, in Cameroon's pursuit of national development through indigenous culture, education and language.

Language In Cameroon, 1960-1990: Bilingual Policy, Multilingual Practice

Cameroon's constitution of 1 October 1961 declares French and English to be the nation's two official languages. Nothing since then has altered that text or challenged or elaborated it by legal or by constitutional processes.[1] But against this bilingual *policy* must be placed what is surely one of Africa's most kaleidoscopic linguistic *practices.*

There are roughly 12,000,000 Cameroonians. They use close to 240 languages, drawn from three major African language families (the Niger-Congo, Afro-Asiatic and Nilo-Saharan, in descending order of the number of their Cameroonian variants), as well as the Indo-European legacy of early trade experience and colonization (a distinctive Cameroon Pidgin, German, French, English). This diversity respects few boundaries. Languages like Arabic and Fulfulde continue to link northerners across the Sahel's ancient political, commercial, and cultural networks, despite the past century's creation of colonial and national borders. Within Cameroon, branches of perhaps the most widely used fully indigenous language, Bamileke, function on both sides of the internal divide separating the nominally 75-80 percent French and 20-25 percent English language domains. Other major indigenous languages (such as Ewondo and Duala) compete where their peoples' homelands and diaspora mingle. As one more example, Cameroon Pidgin has moved from coast to hinterland into not only the anglophone territory but also into substantial pockets among the francophones, and is now reckoned to be the most widely *spoken* language of all. And finally, more than twenty of the 236 purely indigenous languages have achieved standardized written form, especially since 1975, and another seventy are approaching that goal.[2]

Given this uniquely diverse legacy of indigenous complexity and three colonialisms (German, French, British), Cameroon's languages offer scholars and policy-makers a case study as absorbing and instructive as any to be found in Africa. The situation thirty years

8

after independence, despite the constitution's simple formulation, is not just linguistically but politically fractious. The interests attached to language use are fundamental. Individually, who gets what from adding to a personal repertoire? Collectively, what is at stake for the state apparatus in the convergence zone of bilingual policy and multilingual practice, and for social formations in the resource allocation that language as a key marker of ethnicity in this plural society can substantially determine? There are significant fault lines, which make evidence from Cameroon compelling for all those interested in how language issues shape public life and statecraft in contemporary Africa.

But Cameroon, surprisingly in light of this linguistic profile, is seldom encountered in the global scholarship.[3] The empirically rich texts written or edited by Joshua Fishman, one of the major advocates and practitioners of multilingual and multicultural study since the 1950s, draw virtually nothing from Cameroon. Yet this national experience affords a vital case study for those scholars who create written from spoken languages, the theorists of language acquisition, the methodologists and practitioners of language teaching, and the planners of language policy.

With regard to language policy, Cameroon is a natural testing ground for the debate between bilingual and multilingual policy advocates."[4] Given Cameroon's need to declare for bilingualism at independence, policy strategists identified the priority of a state apparatus in which the bilingual adepts shared power and moved to project that partnership into the nation's future, on the grounds of its promise for national unity. The other, mainly indigenous languages were left to their own devices, with minimal long-term prospects as factors in the polity, managed and contained within the official bilingual framework. They nevertheless have found supporters in recent years, with significant claims advanced for indigenous languages as resources worth developing, indeed requiring promotion. Less strategically focused on the instrumental workings of statecraft, more concerned with development and empowerment throughout society, advocacy on this front has stressed local

9

languages primarily as channels for cultures and communities valued in themselves, and additionally functional as linguistic springboards to the two European languages that are necessary for national and global communication.

This multilingual strategy is determinedly pluralistic, keyed to domestic, development-oriented opportunity structures beyond the étatist confines of (putatively) bilingual elites, aligned to more distant, even foreign, interests and agendas. This approach dates back in Africanist policy literature at least to UNESCO's 1951 conference addressing the language issue for incipient new nations, at the same time as Fishman began his investigations.[5] His 1985 formulation, directed in global terms against the hegemonic roles of previously French and now English language and culture, is useful as a guide to current multilingual voices in Cameroon:

it is precisely the smaller, rarer wisdoms that have the greatest and the most overlooked potentials for providing the new and startling insights and perspectives needed if humanity is to be saved. Ultimately, only a multilingual mankind will be able to set aside its parochial biases and view reality from a variety of tentative perspectives.[6]

These are the forces deployed and debates generated. To analyze the emergence and assess the magnitude of these issues during Cameroon's first thirty years of national history, and to appraise the efforts to balance and manage them, are the dual purposes of this study. Progressively greater emphasis will be accorded the multilingual discourse and experimentation that frame Cameroon's currently most vigorous linguistic enterprise. The first focus is, however, some quite recent evidence outside the narrowly linguistic arena, recounted to demonstrate how central language is to any consideration of the Cameroon experience.

An Experiential Profile

To scan the most widely circulated, government-sponsored newspaper, the *Cameroon Tribune,* published six times weekly in French and twice weekly in English, is to grasp immediately the salience of the language issue in Cameroon, indeed its demonstrably central place in public consciousness.[7] Consider, for example, the English edition of 3 March 1989 with its *Weekender* section, eight pages long. Of its forty columns, twelve were devoted to articles successively entitled "The Power of Pidgin English in Cameroon," "It Pays to be Bilingual," and "The Future of English Language." This was a more concentrated burst than a representative sample of popular weekend journalism, but it serves nicely as preface to this coverage of a topic that is sensitive in Cameroon yet obsessively cultivated.

For less casual evidence of the language issue, its complexity, and its human consequences, two episodes are instructive. We first consider Christraud Geary's account of a North West Province, i.e., anglophone court case in 1978.[8] The linguistic and legal details emerged from a dispute about whether a man in his early twenties and a fourteen- year-old girl, whose sexual encounter was not contested, were in fact married according to either customary or modern Cameroon civil law. The verdict potentially affected property rights, parentage, and maintenance and support responsibilities, viewed quite differently within the two frameworks of understanding.

The girl's father, literate in English and a former local council secretary in the village of Wum, brought the complaint against the young man, who had not gone beyond primary school and now worked selling kerosene near Wum Market. The trial evidence and Geary's observations indicated his use of Pidgin and the local language of Wum. The father aimed higher for the daughter.

At trial, language use most clearly measured the distance between the court's environment and the young man's capacity and experience. The court president was a fluent anglophone from the coast, on circuit to a hinterland area he considered "backward." The

11

state prosecutor was a recent product of the Ecole Normale d'Administration et de Magistrature (Yaounde), a bilingually fluent francophone. Both spoke Pidgin, but rejected its demeaning use. The court's registrar and clerk were anglophone, while the two interpreters rendered Pidgin and Wum freely into English but the reverse (Geary implies) only intermittently, when discourse would otherwise have faltered. Linguistically hapless, the defendant had no counsel and called no witnesses beyond the girl's family. He therefore suffered the legal consequences of his confused and shifting testimony, general ignorance of the court's protocol, and its officers' indifference and intimidation.

Found guilty according to modern statute, he was given six years hard labor for "indecency to a girl under 16 years." Geary recounted his post-sentence reaction: "The young man is astonished and still doesn't quite seem to understand what has happened," for he believed himself and the girl to be in "process of marriage" by local custom.[9] So, in their early testimony, later contradicted, did she and her mother, a country woman whose own literacy was confined to speech in Wum.

The story is a classic grassroots demonstration of what is at stake in Cameroon language use, planning, and policy. It pitted a professional elite operating by modern statute, activated by an educated plaintiff who was well acquainted with judicial process, against a semi-literate youth, totally ignorant of the state's legal apparatus and procedures. Although capable of speech in the courtroom's only common working language, Pidgin, the other principals were reluctant to use it. The court begrudged the use of Pidgin and Wum because of the rank and status "marker" they conveyed. The defendant, confined to "country" language use, was passive and ultimately a spectator, not a participant, as his immediate future was sealed. Different prestige values and domains of usage for the languages at issue influenced, perhaps determined the nature of the "justice" handed down. Language demarcated the norms of ethnicity and class within the framework of the modern state apparatus.

The discrepancies revealed between the languages, educations, and ultimately cultures present in Wum's High Court indicate the shapes and nuances of the forces that must inform any study of Cameroon language policy and use, and their relationship to national development. A more public and precisely political demonstration of the language issue's volatility surfaced a decade later, in Cameroon's most striking architectural and political showcase, Yaounde's Palais de Congrès. Dr. Georges Ngango, by all accounts one of President Paul Biya's closest friends and advisors and since 1986 Cameroon's minister of education, had assembled hundreds of his ministerial officials for a highly publicized "Etats Généraux" on education, 24-28 April 1989.[10] It transpired by mid-week that recurrent suspicions among anglophones were fanned once again, as the conference activity moved to include "harmonization" of the national curriculum and exam structure. This is *the* flashpoint between Cameroon's two official language communities. Many of the anglophone minority's intelligentsia, with considerable popular backing in the South West and North West Provinces, perceive schools and the access they provide abroad to English-language higher education and culture as their region's bulwark of autonomy against francophone hegemony. Absorb the schools, it is argued, and full assimilation is inevitable. Stubborn resistance has been the historical pattern and 1989 proved no exception.

By Thursday April 27, the police and army were placed on alert against public demonstrations in the two anglophone provinces, and school principals were dispatched back from Yaounde to keep the peace on those campuses with student bodies old enough to breach it.

The next day was extraordinary. Dr. Ngango, while fielding a question at the Palais podium, was tapped on the shoulder. He followed his interjector off-stage as the national mid-day radio newscast simultaneously announced his dismissal from the cabinet. A ministerial deputy closed the conference with minimal courtesies, offering none of the customary ceremonial or substantive resolutions. The politics of language in its most volatile setting, with "harmonization" perceived as the euphemism for schools to be realigned within the francophone orbit, thus claimed its most prominent victim so far. The styles and policy structures of two school systems in Cameroon, separated by languages and only partly bridged through bilingual experiments to be discussed below, maintain their abrasive history.[11]

Such are the specific episodes that dramatize Cameroon's language experience, disclosing tenacious interests and differential opportunities at work in sensitive arenas of daily human contact and in high politics. Such are the general settings of study and policy debate in the field of language, which align Cameroon's experience with the international literature as a key case study. They reflect linguistic developments in the century and a half since the first mission school opened in 1844, followed in 1885 by German colonization and the first governmentally enforced language policy in Cameroon. A brief survey of this history will frame our major concern, which is to analyze the convergence of language, education, and development policy issues since independence and unification of the French and British trust territories in 1960-1961, and to assess national statecraft in these areas and its impact on the wider society.

Language Use and Policy, 1844-1961

The documentary history of language as a resource and an issue in Cameroon began in 1844 when Baptists introduced missions and then schools. This added language instruction, primarily in English, to the traders' Pidgin long utilized on and near the Cameroon coast. German forms of treaty and occupation from 1885 introduced the first concentrated European language influence. But language policy, though asserting the primacy of German, at first accommodated the various missions' efforts to teach indigenous languages as vehicles for gospel purposes. After 1900, however, two factors reduced that latitude: a more insistent uniformity in all facets of German colonial policy; and an expressed concern that the room made for the indigenous languages of the Duala on the coast and the Bali upcountry was permitting these two major German allies to absorb other Cameroonians' trade and culture. This threatened an ethnic domination that could be troublesome to public order, indeed to the peace that Germany had enforced.[12]

Following the German surrender to Britain and France in 1916, and the League of Nations mandates which followed, British Cameroon experienced relaxation of the more exclusive late German policy. Missions were considered the appropriately low-cost, low- risk channels for the rudimentary level of schooling allotted this distant territory, which remained for thirty more years an administrative adjunct of Nigeria and was largely ignored by colonial economic planners and investors. French Cameroon, by contrast, was more aggressively commercialized, "mobilized" in its labor force, "serviced" with roads and railways. It received a correspondingly larger measure of formal primary education, enforced by the distinctively centralized and francolingual direct rule methods. There were pragmatic concessions for rural mission schools to maintain local languages as vehicles of instruction (though never as subjects in their own right) in the very earliest grades. But Stumpf's careful study of language policy, the ranking source for French Cameroon before 1960, verified that Cameroonians brought within the French educational and linguistic orbit increasingly experienced a "straight for French" policy.[13]

Language policy became notably complex in 1960-1961 when the former British and French parts of Cameroon joined in a federal republic, as the West and East states respectively. The constitution was deceptively simple in its one clause touching language: "The official languages of the Federal Republic of Cameroon shall be French and English." This bilingualism rescued anglophones in West Cameroon from French language control over both English and the local languages that the British had fostered. But options were narrow. The referendum process that replaced British administration never offered independence or its corollary, linguistic self-determination, as a feature of sovereignty. It was either federation with francophones in Cameroon, or with Nigeria. The latter situation would likely have meant a language experience combining official English with a varied use of indigenous languages (and perhaps Igbo, Ibibio, and Efik, depending on internal administrative boundaries, for Nigerian migration and commercial interests were strong). Conditions would have resembled Nigeria's "Middle Belt." There, small ethnic groups persistently seek, through federal political channels, to limit more powerful ethnic influences by promoting both English and their own languages as counterweights (a circumstance some Cameroon anglophones might now prefer as the lesser hurdle). [14]

Bilingual Policy since 1961

As it was, the boundary and constitutional arrangements of 1961 created their own distinctive language map for Cameroon. The combination of official bilingualism and the maintenance of primary education as a state rather than federal domain kept local languages and English active in West Cameroon's schools and society at large. A United Republic replaced the federation in 1972. There had already been administrative adjustments aligning West Cameroon's education system to the East's; all education now became a central government responsibility. But the schools and languages of the former West Cameroon, far from disappearing, became anglophones' most distinct regional interest and rallying point against assimilation. The consequences included problems, opportunities, and a range of speculation, research and policy choices, that are unique on the continent.[15]

The key voice in the bargaining on languages in 1961 and on language policy matters for the next decade was Dr. Bernard Fonlon, whom we can utilize to introduce the intricacy of education, language, and culture in Cameroon ever since. Arguably the most broadly educated Cameroonian of his day, Fonlon was a Catholic Anglophone from one of Africa's most intensely varied ethnic landscapes, the Kumbo area of the North West Province Grassfields.[16] He acquired a vast array of training and experience through early schooling at Kumbo and Sasse College (Buea), seminary in Nigeria, and university education in Paris, Oxford, and Cork, where he completed a doctorate at the National University of Ireland in 1961 with a dissertation on black poetics, written in French. We may usefully reckon him within the strategic generation of young men in their thirties throughout Africa's dependencies who prepared independence in the 1950s and were given opportunities, once it was achieved, to put their talents to work.

But quite special circumstances attended Fonlon. He had been a young seminarian denied ordination on its very threshold because of his Afrocentric cultural bent, who then undertook a special calling for

17

service as a layman instead of a priest (all sources stress the asceticism and probity that embellished his sense of duty). He acquired Latin as well as the modern languages his ports of study call required, and in particular mastered French, once he realized in his late twenties its likely bearing on his own, his people's, and any future Cameroon's prospects. His Paris connections with *Présence Africaine* made him a unique bridge between Cameroon's two European language intelligentsias. He displayed commanding talents among his Cameroon age peers (especially the anglophones), who formed a relatively small band moving as students from both British and French areas to universities in Ibadan, Dakar, and beyond.

Incidental, but worth noting, are two final points, touching Fonlon's autonomy: the first years of Cameroon's independence and Fonlon's real influence coincided with Pope John XXIII's leadership in Rome and the powerful non-sectarian energies of ecumenical Catholicism; and Fonlon was not compromised by partisan politics while a student abroad in the late 1950s. He was later very politically active but was no mere "party man" or anyone's temperamental or intellectual subordinate. These circumstances in church and state enabled Fonlon to join the fledgling political leadership and to exercise his skills and calling in extraordinary ways in Cameroon's early years of independence.

Fonlon's language agenda, reflecting his broader culture, has defined that of Cameroon ever since. It was meant fundamentally to translate the even-handed constitutional bilingualism between the majority francophones and the minority anglophones into practice, securing anglophone rights, leaving no official place for indigenous languages. These latter were of course the staple of preschool infancy and much the widest in general lifelong use for most citizens. But the most distant horizons, not just the immediate landscape, shaped Fonlon's language policy, which in principle offered a highly ambitious, even visionary scheme of social engineering. Cameroon, known for its linguistic diversity, was to become a model for the entire continent's benefit by reconciling its dual colonial legacy and clearing a bilingual track to the fullest possible measure of modem

18

global usage in English and French.

The key document on both the domestic and continental fronts was a long article, "A Case for Early Bilingualism," published during 1963 in the fourth number of the journal *Abbia,* which Fonlon inaugurated when government and UNESCO funds established it as Cameroon's essential forum of scholarship and cultural commentary. It was to remain the most constant source of his influence through its two decades of publication, spanning Fonlon's series of governmental appointments until 1971 and his later "grey eminence" roles which followed naturally from his gifts. This 1963 essay adopted a premise for domestic purposes consonant with Fonlon's views and experiences, that language was a definitive characteristic of education and culture in Cameroon, indeed the key to its political culture:

> it is the indispensable instrument for the furtherance of mental growth, of intellectual development, in each and every one of us…it also enlivens the common experience that the people in question have garnered from the impact of their surroundings, the memory of their fathers, their common experiences in time as a polity…language is a very powerful investment in forging national unity. Today, when all the insistence is on science and technology, so much harping on the overwhelming importance of language will strike some as a startling irrelevance…But … there is…an essential foundation to be laid in language as an indispensable preparation for any further studies.[17]

Thus, from the early stages of Cameroon's nationhood the fabric of public debate about its nature was substantially aligned with the language issue, an enduring theme echoed a quarter-century later in the *Cameroon Tribune* material cited above.

What Fonlon advocated was clear, if difficult to implement. Lacking the reality or the prospect of a common indigenous language for Cameroon, to his "very deep regret," the "primordial role of language" would need to be satisfied by "the languages once imposed upon us by our colonial masters, the languages that were once the instrument of our humiliation." Only Arabic showed any immediate, more indigenous promise for "modern technological progress," but "development cannot wait" for any domestic or quasi-domestic candidate.[18]

Thus, in Cameroon, the English and French languages should be jointly and equivalently nurtured. This should happen not just in the formal but limited sense already adopted by the constitutional provision for official bilingualism, with each language continuing to prevail on its old terrain, linked through the bilingual proficiency of an elite in public life. Fonlon instead called for "individual bilingualism" and the use of Cameroon schools to make certain that "every child that passes through our education system shall be able to speak and write both English and French." Defending the ambitious scope of the plan, he cited the deliberate revival of ancient Hebrew to serve Israel's needs, to unify the peoples of its returned diaspora and provide them a modern scientific and technical vocabulary. If Israel could start the process with its kindergartens, so "the teaching of English and French together, here in Cameroon, should start right from the very first day that the child takes his seat in the infant school."[19]

The text acknowledged the indigenous languages of Cameroon's homes and workplaces, but left the responsibility for their survival to the preschool home and assigned them no place in the school curricula of this earliest, most sweeping language policy proposal for Cameroon. Instead, to bolster the previous acquisition of French and English, Fonlon recommended options in Latin and Greek (recalling his own experience and tastes) for secondary education. The channels carved for English and French should be planned as parallels, so that students reaching the newly established federal university would achieve parity and the state would not incur the costs of a linguistically "double university with a double faculty" like Belgium's Louvain.[20]

Such were Fonlon's specific ambitions for Cameroon. But there were still wider dimensions of the policy. He considered Cameroon uniquely qualified and poised for a bilingual experiment of more than national significance. Other bilingual nations experienced more competition than they could easily absorb. Only Canada sustained the same two languages as Cameroon, with all the opportunities that English and French offered in the international domains of business, science, and diplomacy, but there, as in the cognate bilingual settings of Belgium and South Africa, historical antagonisms divide the language communities and made cooperation problematic at best.

Cameroon, he asserted, had no such historical and emotional contradictions to overcome - French and English were not "organic" languages - and could mobilize joint ventures for its national benefit, indeed for Africa's benefit as a whole. Cameroon's proper cultivation of bilingualism could provide, in time and at costs he urged his country to face and surmount, "our noble mission, our special pride and privilege," i.e.,Cameroon's leadership in an African unity forged in substantial part by bold language initiatives against the prevailing "African Babel." Cameroon as a sentinel state for modern pan-African development through bilingualism was Fonlon's broad and urgent vision in the republic's early years.[21]

The objective, then, was to activate the bilingual framework of Cameroon's constitution so that domestic language policy would also become pivotal for Africa at large. But Fonlon's vision was in fact not realized and was only sporadically addressed, as a variety of research findings made clear. The most systematic investigation of Cameroon language use, planned and undertaken between 1975 and 1978 and published in 1983, indicated the bilingual policy's shortfall, indeed the stubborn resistance of usage against policy.[22] A research team of thirty surveyed 4850 households in all but one of Cameroon's thirty-one largest cities and towns, representing 28.5 percent of the urban population, precisely the settings where educational preparation for employment and the linguistic feedback from schools and jobs might be expected to register a significant bilingual imprint. But little impact from Fonlon's policy was discernible fifteen years after its articulation, i.e., as the cohorts who entered schools as his views became active approached maturity. The paper dealing with bilingualism's relationship to education, based on

21

nearly 13,000 school-age children, showed that 87 percent of those in francophone Cameroon were speaking French and 72 percent in anglophone Cameroon were speaking Standard English (not Pidgin). But for the "cross-over" effect of Fonlon's vision, French speech in anglophone areas, English speech in francophone areas, the absolute numbers were so slight as to be statistically insignificant - there were mere dozens of such youngsters, not hundreds or thousands.[23]

Yet again contrary to bilingual initiatives was the continued salience of indigenous rather than European speech. Fulfulde dominated much of the north. Pidgin dominated anglophone Cameroon and played a role in francophone pockets near the pre-1961 boundaries and on the (francophone) Douala coast. French and Ewondo were both widely spoken in much of the south, radiating from Yaounde. French was accorded some potential for spreading, Standard English none. One more finding contradicted Fonlon's model trajectory for language acquisition (mother tongue to primary official language to secondary official language): the most likely sequences were revealed to be mother tongue to Pidgin to French or Standard English, or mother tongue to Fulfulde to French.[24]

No subsequent large-scale longitudinal study has since confirmed what these data suggest. But there is little doubt from the available literature that kaleidoscopic, substantially indigenous language use has frustrated official bilingual policy in Cameroon, where the use of English and French languages maintains largely parallel, non-convergent, monolingual tracks within their former colonial domains.

More recent research by Ekane confirms any visitor's observation: where there *is* evidence of Fonlon's vision shaping language experience in Cameroon, to utilize the "institutional bilingualism" among "those dispensing assigned government services ... one conducts official business in French or English," not both, the choice being determined by the old borders. [25] Ekane studied a prime source for those officials, one of the major initiatives funded and sustained from Fonlon's time, the Bilingual Grammar School (BGS) founded in 1963 and now situated in Buea. He surveyed the campus and analyzed responses from 429 graduates among those trained

22

there, between 1976 and 1986, to be the public servants, translators and interpreters who would constitute bilingualism's vanguard. [26]

Ekane found an environment that has significantly fostered sympathy between its anglophone and francophone students and assisted them in subsequent schooling and occupations. The BGS anglophones, for instance, did not generally need to invest the notorious extra year of residence their non-BGS counterparts usually require to attune themselves to French as the dominant language of instruction at the University of Yaounde. Class sizes, however, were twice in 1984 what they had been a decade earlier, making "immersion" as against less effective "second language" teaching strategy difficult to utilize. The more active skills of speech and writing lagged in success rates behind more passive listening and reading. External French and English exam performances in the school were lower in its second than in its first decade. BGS, designed to create an official bilingual cadre, was an increasingly costly resource, needing substantial remedy and reconstruction after a quarter-century. [27]

Resource constraints were and are an issue, and Fonlon had admitted that the "start- up" costs of bilingualism would be heavy. The needs generated by any bilingual school like BGS, such as special teacher training, multiple sets of materials and exams, and the extra costs for planning and implementation, are in Cameroon compounded by the fact of two official *European* languages. [28] The intricacy of the scheme and its expenses were bound to tax its practitioners and stretch Cameroon's resources.

The more sympathetic Cameroonian scholar-critics of language policy who have surveyed the nation's bilingual effort and its legacy have cast what they perceive as its failure in the light of the politics prevailing at and since independence. [29] Consider Chumbow's comprehensive 1980 review of language developments after two decades of independence. As against the ideal of its leadership for Africa, Chumbow wrote that Cameroon's English-French bilingual policy "was simply dictated by pragmatism" as an aspect of political compromise which (far from leading Africa) was a calculated, lowest-common-denominator effort to keep the Cameroon federation intact, "the most expedient solution... both necessary and justifiable as a *temporary measure.*"[30] Two larger facts of life, Chumbow argued, "stifled" Fonlon's ideal: the Francophone majority of 75 percent that could take or leave English sapped all initiatives for interlocking parity and symmetry; Cameroon's state builders, dominated by francophones, sought the closer union finally achieved by referendum in 1972, rather than the federal autonomy and decentralization in some areas that anglophone initiatives represented. Fonlon's influence as theorist therefore never translated much into practice.

Chumbow's survey of bilingual achievements since 1961 stressed their modest limits: translations of conferences and texts within the constraints of the experts' numbers and capacities; substantial efforts throughout the education system to offer both languages which fell far short of effecting convergence of the parallel paths; extra-curricular schemes directed mainly to the second language skills of civil servants and the adult population at large (which remained largely urban and prohibitively expensive, although radio outreach registered some success). There were some genuine examples of a bilingual will, but mixed achievements at best. In summary,

There has never been a government blue-print with a specific timetable of expected achievements in bilingualism over the years, comparable to the various "development plans" that emphasize economic and political development projects...[there was] no clear knowledge of the destination of English-French bilingualism in Cameroon and consequently no clear knowledge of the best way to get there. [31]

Less sympathetic was Tchoungui, because of her specific focus not only on the tepid compromise and wasteful costs of official Eurocentric bilingualism in educational terms, but also on the policy's morbid impact on national development in the broadest sense. She wrote in 1983:

bilingualism in Cameroon – at least the type advocated by

24

official proponents – is still more a wish than a reality. [Survey data] are also a measure of the financial waste and burden that bilingual institutions have become for the country.[32]

She then turned more trenchant, to attack an original mistake, charging that the cost problem was willfully compounded by "a cultural sin by omission" of mother tongues and by subservience to the language interests of the former colonial powers, especially the French. The result was "Cameroon's failure twenty years after Independence to achieve some measure of self-reliance and identity... a remarkable inability to live or to think out of well trodden colonial tracks." She considered it unlikely that Cameroon's language planning would "draw the Home Languages from the background into the foreground ... as in other African countries.[33]

In light of these materials on bilingualism in practice and a brief scan of Fonlon's career after 1972, one can perceive his own considerable frustration over Cameroon's languishing bilingualism. Intensely active in the politics of the first decade of independence -- as chief of mission at the presidency 1961-1964, then a parliamentarian and minister of transport 1968-1970 and minister of health 1970-1971 -- Fonlon left office late in 1971, well short of his fiftieth birthday, and devoted the next decade until his full retirement to *Abbia* and the University of Yaounde's Department of African Literature. The timing of his departure from government was significant, for the 1972 change to a unitary republic was a watershed experience for the anglophones who had participated in the creation of Cameroon.

The new structure absorbed all powers previously reserved to the two states. It stiffened anglophone views, making schools a key point to defend on grounds of autonomy. And it changed Fonlon. Although he remained on central committees of the ruling party until his death in 1986, he was using academic speeches by the mid-1970s to denounce the indifference of the francophone majority to his crucial language principle, bilingual parity. In 1979, citing the spread of English world-wide, stating "that I no longer believe in the equality of the two languages," he called in *Abbia,* very much his voice, for English as " the first language of instruction in the University; indeed…the first official Language of Cameroon." The intractable nature of the national language issue was aptly reflected in this, the most determined bilingual advocate's ultimate judgment.[34]

There were alternative approaches to Fonlon's from the start. Two were formulated in early issues of *Abbia.* The anglophone scholar-diplomat Kisob argued in 1964 that Cameroon Pidgin, already widely spoken, was a candidate for wider national and official language recognition, and this position still has advocates in 1990.[35] The Wum court case described above, however, suggests that Pidgin lacks legitimacy among its anglophone users, and its spread to francophone Cameroon has perhaps inherent and insurmountable limits, despite evidence of its "border zone" use. Another scheme advanced in 1964 was the francophone linguist Ngijol's, for a commission to choose among indigenous languages the one most promising as an official language, and then to facilitate the switch of support from all others, including French and English, to the chosen standard. But this proposal was as problematic as Fonlon's, or even more so, given the constitution's bilingualism, Cameroon's federal character at that time, and the need for the Cameroon state to avoid the appearance and substance of favoritism toward one ethnic group's interests over others'. To advance Ewondo (the language Ngijol suggested as the likeliest candidate) against Duala, for instance, risked political peace, if not secessionist challenge. Ngijol himself in 1978 modified and in 1989 renounced this approach.[36]

Cameroon's language situation around 1980, then, resembled the patchwork that Chumbow described. The compromise between anglophone and francophone elites on bilingual grounds since 1961 turned out badly enough on grounds of both policy and practice to alienate its chief architect, Fonion. Nothing emerged that was more likely to succeed than his bilingualism. Its implementation by government had reached an impasse and the country proved indifferent even before Fonlon repudiated his creation. Language

26

policy and the national language experience were mutually incompatible, and moving farther apart. Committed to not just one but two European languages, the government's priorities were confused and its resources were inadequate to support its own policy, let alone for any attention to sporadically promoted indigenous language alternatives.

The 1980s, however, have witnessed developments more linguistically interesting and more policy-sensitive than previous efforts. One is a multilingual option most closely identified with the University of Yaounde's Department of African Languages and Linguistics. Its program makes Cameroon a primary focus for all parties interested in African languages and their policy implications for education and culture as well as language. It is a striking initiative, which keys our further discussion of Cameroon language policy in the recent past and present - and its prospects for the 1990s and beyond.

Multilingualism in theory

Two pivotal figures, Emmanuel Chia and Maurice Tadadjeu, joined forces in the department in 1977, combining experiences and interests well suited for the enterprise. Chia, an anglophone from Kom, North West Province, and Tadadjeu, a francophone from Dschang, West Province, had both studied linguistics at Georgetown University earlier in the decade, Chia working on a doctorate there, Tadadjeu on a master's prior to the doctoral program at University of Southern California. By 1977, Chia was head of department at Yaounde and Tadadjeu was that year's faculty appointment. They created a formidable collaboration within the department, which helped shape and was placed at the disposal of the wider network of activity to be described below. It was augmented in 1985 by Beban Chumbow, the Bamenda anglophone noted above, returning to Cameroon as the department's professor after many years at the University of Ilorin (Nigeria). They combined many strengths: specialist training in linguistics that Fonlon (for all his gifts) lacked; balance between their anglophone and francophone backgrounds, and a scholarly apparatus for and predisposition toward indigenous language research and its application more available from the English-speaking, USA-based graduate training all three received than French-oriented universities would have provided.[37]

Tadadjeu's scholarship was first off the mark. Articles published during his post-graduate career established his position and anticipated the ground he was to stake out in his further writings and intensively active practitioner's role between his return home in 1977 and roughly 1985. This period is our immediate focus; more recent work carries Tadadjeu the linguist into the domain of social philosophy and will be examined in the conclusion.

A key 1975 paper began with an assessment of the first decade of official Cameroonian bilingualism, and covered much the same retrospective ground as Chumbow's 1980 paper cited above, concluding that the two languages had become more firmly entrenched in their own areas, spreading only feebly across the

28

colonial linguistic boundary. The government's "line of least resistance" policy for knitting together the language communities was not well served, any more than were Fonlon's Pan-African ambitions, now increasingly derelict. Only a tiny elite managed both languages adequately. The policy as enacted might be serviceable to the state's survival interest, but it consumed inordinate resources at social costs not justified by the results (this analysis was the heart of a 1977 paper), while the political risks of language as a wedge instead of a bridge would have at some point to be reckoned with. [38]

The solution Tadadjeu outlined in 1975 and has elaborated ever since did not discard Fonlon or destroy the bilingual approach; Tadadjeu was, and remains, no abolitionist of English and French. He recognized that European bilingualism was *necessary* in Cameroon, accepting Fonlon's premise that there was no indigenous "wider communication" language candidate for national and international purposes in the near future, but urged the admission that it was not *sufficient*. English and French, while retained, must be situated within the practical context of a vastly multilingual population's customary usage, and room in schools and resources elsewhere must be allocated to the development of certain indigenous languages in appropriate domains. Without relinquishing the constitution's compromise or Fonlon's ideal for Cameroon's leadership in African language issues, Tadadjeu argued for complementarity between bilingualism and a fresh multilingual initiative. "Trilingualisme extensif," the term he coined in a key 1985 paper, offered Cameroon a realigned strategy for language development, more effective than bilingualism on its own. [39]

If some 236 indigenous languages still held their place on the speech map of a population still 75 percent rural, Tadadjeu argued, this reality must influence the approach to sound linguistic policy in Cameroon. These languages need not be impediments to "rational" planning; rather, they were resources to be selectively developed. Although common sense and experience with local languages elsewhere in the twentieth-century world have proved that not all were serviceable and that many would in time disappear, others could

29

be usefully cultivated. Criteria were established and applied as early as 1979, when a standard alphabet for Cameroon's languages came into use. Constantly reformulated, these criteria dealt with the number of speakers (10,000 were needed for written texts to be viably produced for schools and other markets), the proximity and thus the threat of larger languages with absorptive capacities (mainly indigenous in rural areas, European in the larger cities), and the potential for promoting standardization within neighboring "clusters" of dialects and languages for the purpose of creating written conventions.[40]

Like Fonlon's program for bilingualism, Tadadjeu's from the start identified schools as the crucial arena for trilingualism. Specifically, "a Cameroon trilingual education system should aim at helping each Cameroonian student become *fluent and literate* in his mother tongue or a related provincial language [i.e., a "langue véhiculaire"] as well as in the two official languages.[41]

Most obviously a strategy for language repertoire expansion, the scheme also entailed significant alterations and additions for the established school routines, the most critical settings. Instruction in early primary grades, for example, would begin through an indigenous language and then add an official language, thus removing the hurdle of an alien language medium in students' first encounter with schools. Then, with indigenous reading, writing, and counting skills in place, instruction in an official language would start with speech (English or French, geographically determined) before moving to the more formal skills, and the second official language instruction would follow in upper primary or lower secondary school. The exact blend and sequence of transfer could vary, for instance, between rural and urban schools. In secondary schools, the German and Spanish still being taught and examined among francophones should give way to indigenous vehicular languages (that was the hope expressed in 1975; Tadadjeu would note the retention of German and Spanish in 1981 and call for their removal in 1985). At the tertiary level, the University of Yaounde and various "grandes écoles," as their contributions, would include advanced level study in languages, linguistics, and educational strategies geared at the apex of the system

30

to sustain research and teaching momentum for the indigenous languages. Such a policy model would in fact aim for "quadrilinguisme" for the truly advanced learners, with baccalauréat level francophones and GCE "A" level anglophones competent to speak, read, and write both official languages and both a vehicular and mother tongue indigenous language in their appropriate domains.[42]

But it was the language competence of all Cameroonians, not just those with higher education, that most concerned Tadadjeu and his associates. His comprehensive version of "trilinguisme extensif" accordingly called by 1985 for two dimensions of linguistic policy integration. A "horizontal" linkage would provide any two Cameroonians the facility to communicate orally on first contact through official and/or vehicular languages ("la possibilité ... d'utiliser une même langue pour communiquer dès leur première rencontre"). A "vertical" component would secure a new and crucial element of his plan, as he now moved from the vocabulary of languages as resources to the linguistic *right* of each citizen to maternal language competence, in both linguistic and cultural senses ("ses droits linguistiques et en conséquence, de participer efficacement au développement socioculturel de sa communauté de langue maternelle").[43]

As fully articulated by 1985, the policy of "trilingualisme extensif" clarified an issue left ambiguous and potentially troublesome in 1981, when Tadadjeu appeared to confer rights of maintenance and security on 236 indigenous languages. This was an unwieldy and practicably insupportable number. Tadadjeu in 1985 estimated that roughly 100 were viable on grounds of utility for enough people as a written language ("sous la forme standard, i.e., comme vecteurs quotidiens d'une communication écrite"), and that fifty of these were likely to become permanent in the spoken national repertoire. As of 1990, some twenty indigenous languages had achieved a standard written form and seventy more approached that stage of development. [44]

There was one final dimension to Tadadjeu's design for what he called "le profil linguistique idéal du Camerounais." We have noted

31

his claim, first, that indigenous languages were *resources,* then that they constituted a set of *rights* considered as natural and fundamental because they were vehicles of culture, historically and authentically rooted. He argued additionally in 1985 for the allocation of resources to add to the Cameroonian languages' stock of scientific and technical vocabulary, so that they would serve the same needs that French and English had come to satisfy:

> The cultural functions of our languages has (sic) already been assumed to a large degree...the problem is only to give these languages and their speakers the necessary abilities for their improved operation in the modem context, i.e., essentially scientific and technological.[45]

It should be noted (again) that this effort did *not* entail any deconstruction of French and English, given their global status and their prestige values for those Cameroonians already vested with their command and those still wishing to acquire them. Rather, indigenous languages would serve as bridges to them and would be raised to *their* levels of expressive competence.

"Trilingualisme extensif" thus built the case for parity ("complémentarité fonctionelle") between indigenous and European languages. National development needs for all Cameroonians could not otherwise be addressed. Tadadjeu had struck this note just before his return home in 1977:

> we need to keep in mind the general goal of educational planning in Africa today ... to ensure that young people finishing school at least at the primary level adequately fit and effectively contribute to the development of the society .... The purpose of language education planning ... is to help educational authorities in specific countries adopt, plan and implement those language education policies and programs which best prepare specific groups (students or working adults) to properly use specific language skills in specific languages for performing those specific

functions that are required of them by their society. While this is by no means an easy task, it is not an impossible one either.[46]

It now had a theory and policy focus.

Multilingualism in Practice: The Organizational Framework

It goes without saying, as we turn to the implementation of a multilingual program, that this task *is* difficult, suited only for the most determined linguists. There is suspicion about its danger on grounds of ethnic group interest and rivalry. Skepticism can be expected among those it is meant to serve and empower, given the demonstrated structures of opportunity through European languages: "Why me? Why us?" And a shrug of bureaucratic shoulders is a likely enough attitude in circles where a foreign language has already provided access to office. Thus, caution must inform any discussion of Tadadjeu's and his colleagues' efforts, as attention now shifts to the very considerable effort to frame this initiative in Cameroon's public life.

Most of the multilingual activity deployed since 1978 is framed within one major program, the Project of Operational Research for the Teaching of Languages in Cameroon (PROPELCA).[47] Tadadjeu directs its team of twenty researchers; it is designed to operate (funds permitting) until the year 2000. Its most basic element thus far has taken four indigenous languages as media of instruction to start the primary education cycle for more than 3,000 children in eleven schools, mostly rural and all "confessional" (seven other languages are in more preliminary stages of the experiment). The curricular and testing structure is designed both to prove the efficacy of mother tongue education as the best preparation for European language competence and to anchor the mother tongue usage as a lifelong skill. The pattern of instruction year-by-year, utilizing specially prepared texts and teachers for each stage, allocates classroom time between mother tongue (MT) and official language (OL) roughly as follows:

Year	MT time allocation/function	OL time allocation/function
1	75 percent /medium of instruction for all subjects, reading, writing, counting	25 percent /second language subject as conversation
2	60 percent /ditto	40 percent /intro of reading, writing, counting
3	40 percent /ditto, plus orthography, grammar, composition	60 percent /ditto, plus intro as medium of instruction
4-5	20 percent /ditto	80 percent /ditto
6+	5 percent /as subject matter(culture, history, etc)	95 percent /ditto, eventual intro of second OL

Other facets of PROPELCA have not been as substantially fielded as the primary school effort. Adult literacy is the most advanced of these ancillary phases, as it depends more on local initiative than on centrally managed, staffed, and financed sources. Approximately twenty villages throughout southern Cameroon have language committees emphasizing adult indigenous language literacy linked to PROPELCA. They bring together local notables, including elders in traditional office, younger professionals and officials, and linguists, in a support structure that determines the dialect of reference, provides village access to PROPELCA's linguists and teachers, supplements external funding and operates extra-mural efforts. Such committees animate and legitimize the entire

PROPELCA spectrum of activity, from early schooling to adult settings.

PROPELCA's further ambitions require funds not yet secured and therefore lag behind their projected schedules. These include instruction of both indigenous and the two European official languages in secondary schools on firmer pedagogical grounds and the previously noted scheme to develop scientific and technical vocabularies in Cameroon languages.

To advance this work, PROPELCA assembled in the 1980s a broad base of collaboration for linguistic study and its programmatic application in many parts of Cameroon, including agencies with experience gained long before PROPELCA's own creation.[48] There is, for instance, one school that has actively promoted indigenous languages since the 1960s, Douala's Collège Libermann. Most prominently, the evangelical Protestant group Société Internationale de Linguistique (SIL), which entered Cameroon in 1967, operating through government protocols, provides PROPELCA a logistic and technical hub in Yaounde.[49] Ranging far beyond its indigenous gospel translation and publication priorities, SIL's printing facilities, for example, turn out teachers' manuals, students' workbooks, and adult learners' materials in both the official and indigenous languages. Its computers enable the technical staff to create the written forms of indigenous languages and provide general access to the international linguistic scholarship. SIL also provides the Yaounde facilities when PROPELCA stages training seminars and courses for school teachers, principals and administrators. Also parts of the private "confessional" network are the permanent secretariats for Catholic and Protestant instruction in Cameroon. Their schools provide the sites thus far committed to PROPELCA's pilot projects, since state schools (as elaborated below) remain the preserve of official bilingualism. Funds from abroad (especially the Canadian International Development Agency's) have been instrumental in PROPELCA's support network during its first decade.

Domestic public sector support for PROPELCA and the multilingual effort in general include Tadadjeu's two institutional

35

homes, the university's Department of African Languages and Linguistics, and the major ministerial research body, the Institute of Social Sciences. These agencies, constrained by budgets and the minefields of language politics, support advanced study in indigenous languages and channel Cameroon nationals into this research and development network, but the government is cautious about sponsoring this effort, especially its utilization in schools. Still, as one measure of the composite effort generated by PROPELCA and the Cameroon network Tadadjeu and others have created, a comprehensive report published in 1986, covering the integration of indigenous languages with school systems in nineteen francophone African nations, accorded Cameroon the second lengthiest survey. It trailed only Rwanda, where the dominance of KiRwanda makes indigenization policy and practice much easier to pursue.[50]

Multilingualism in Practice: Perspectives from the Field

What this multilingual, indigenously slanted approach entails as its limited resources are fielded can be glimpsed on the cover page of a representative journal for the Ghomala language, and more fully understood through a survey of the rapid evolution of Fe'efe'e since just before independence. Fe'efe'e is a major language in the francophone West and upper Littoral Provinces, prominent within Bamileke society, Cameroon's largest ethnic group. The story runs against the grain of French language dominance, demonstrating indigenous language channels activated before 1960, then augmented as the network efforts spread.

We can trace a classic pattern in Fe'efe'e's emergence from the profile established by sources which include a 1985 bibliography of publications in and about Fe'efe'e.[51] It started in the later 1950s with the Catholic Diocese of Nkongsamba's creation of the Fe'efe'e language committee, Nufi (the word means "something new"), and a series of local publications issued by a Belgian as well as a local Bafang press. This first series included a catechism and selections from the evangelists, and a local priest's simultaneous production of proverbs and scriptural readings. Halfway through the bibliography's list, in 1972, the cumulative publications reflected the move into secular concerns and scholarship and a substantial indigenous publishing industry. Tadadjeu noted in 1975 the study of Fe'efe'e at schools in France as well as at home, and 3,000 literates in Fe'efe'e certificated by Nufi, which in 1981 he called a model for the organization of similar indigenous language programs.[52]

The roster of activity was indeed substantial, well before the Protestants in SIL and then Tadadjeu's PROPELCA augmented the original Catholic Fe'efe'e repertoire. Nufi hadsustained a monthly newsletter since 1958 and individual editions using Fe'efe'e were credited by 1972 with a descriptive grammar, an introductory socio-linguistic survey, a conversation instruction manual, a local map, a more detailed geography text, and a book on hygiene. That year also witnessed the appearance of an American's phonological study of the

37

language from UCLA, SIL's first significant entry. Just as striking as the variety of the materials were their new publication locales: Nkongsamba and Bafang within the region, France, Belgium, and now Los Angeles abroad. The full Fe'efe'e publication history as of 1985 revealed the additional force of SIL's activity and the PROPELCA work, especially by one of Tadadjeu's closest colleagues, Dr. Etienne Sadembouo, on his own linguistic heritage. By 1985 the profile included specialized studies on syntax and grammar, a variety of manuals and guides geared to a Fe'efe'e diploma program now in place, an expanded Catholic repertoire, augmented titles in poetry and geography, a pharmacopoeia, and a Fe'efe'e-French dictionary. Fe'efe'e publications now appeared in Yaounde (at the university, through SIL's regularly updated teaching manuals, and in ministerial circuits) and in Douala. In addition, Nufi sponsored diploma courses in written Fe'efe'e at some sixty sites throughout Cameroon, financing this activity by external funding (75 percent of the total) and its own volunteers' contributions of money as well as time. Student fees covered the classroom furnishings and teaching materials; there was no Nufi teacher salary structure.

By 1990, then, in this especially strong enclave of local interest, the analytic and applied work over thirty years had spread from Catholic priests across denominational lines and created a task force of linguists, teachers, and publishers. It provided Cameroon's research and development workers on indigenous languages a model case history for their practice and their alignment with one of the two European languages.

This long history of Fe'efe'e language development can be compared, perhaps as guide, to newer enterprises of the 1970s and 1980s placed in anglophone Cameroon by Protestant initiatives. We first consider two of the most active and successful cases, the South West Province Mundani, then the North West Province Bafut.

The collaboration of two SIL field based foreign linguists, two Mundani locals they trained, and a "Mundani Linguistic Team" which undertook survey and support work created a written form of Mundani.[53] The first decade's production totalled thirteen items and

38

more than 400 pages of text. Specifically, there were five books of popular miscellaneous readings from traditional sources, two of animal stories and one on musical instruments, alongside the appearance (standard for all such ventures) of a calendar, a songbook, school primers and a lexicon. The Gospel of Luke published and celebrated in March 1989 completed the first decade's cycle of work. The effort was substantial, addressed literacy needs for all ages, and supplied the sources for a secular cultural growth while leading to the publication of Luke.

Not only the project's specific achievements are of interest. The chief linguistic investigator, a SIL staff member, independently published an account of the Mundani project's roots, which very usefully addressed basic questions of motives for indigenous language interest - the "Why me? Why us?" questions locals might well ask either a religious or a secular linguist. Annett in fact characterized first reactions in 1978 among the 23,000 Mundani as "a sense of bewilderment," and summarized a typical response: "Read and write *Mundani?!* Why, it's English we need!" Her reaction was instructive for an appreciation of her own goals as well as the local interests at work:

> They had rightly diagnosed their problem and prescribed its solution. They did need English, the horizontal dimension [for modernization linkages]. It only remained to demonstrate to them that literacy in Mundani would not only be an effective first step towards that goal, but also bring enrichment socially and culturally.[54]

Whose convictions these were, and in what ways they were persuasive, Annett's text left uncertain. But whatever blend of Mundani's own field of aspirations and those brought to the community from outside prevailed at the start in 1978, a study committee was formed, and the project went forward. The decisive finding which gave it sufficient backing and momentum, at a point around 1981 when activity seemed stalled, was that the migrant

Mundani people in southern and western Cameroon's largest cities, not the village population, were the key targets for indigenous literacy efforts. The limits of rural opportunity created Mundani migrant clusters in Buea, Bamenda, Douala, etc., whose material and emotional needs as "strangers" there (so Annett surmised, though her text lacked substantial data) forged an urban ethnic community which renewed the sense of a Mundani heritage endangered by the lethargy of rural circumstances. The urban migrants' Sunday *njangi* meetings (these are known as *tontines* in francophone Cameroon) which pooled investments and renewed hospitality began to include Mundani language training before the normal transactions. With an awareness that "language transmits culture," participants in these urban settings constituted an effective catalyst group for the wider Mundani population. In effect, the work with the village-based language committee shifted to this more transient population as a critical mass, with its comparatively augmented resources and prestige as the keys to a significant expansion in the Mundani publications list by 1985, a bi-monthly newsletter, and the emerging practice of certifying Mundani literates by the time the Gospel of Luke was published in 1989. This is slow work; a 1987 estimate reckoned less than 1 percent Mundani indigenous literacy. But there is a foundation in place and Fe'efe'e suggests the potential.[55]

The second anglophone example, Bafut, is notably collaborative across denominational and organizational lines. There, Joseph Mfonyam, an anglophone Protestant, joined SIL in the 1970s, raised funds both at home and abroad for evangelical work, and simultaneously began advanced linguistic training in Chia's and Tadadjeu's department in Yaounde. Using his own language as the basis of his academic work, Mfonyam distinguished himself in 1989 by completing the senior degree, the Doctorat d'Etat, with a dissertation on tone in Bafut. Meanwhile, in the village, he has placed his SIL and university-based resources at PROPELCA's disposal, organizing the local language committee with support from the fon's palace and crossing confessional lines to supervise the pilot Bafut language program in a Catholic primary school. Outside Bafut,

Mfonyam is on SIL's teaching staff in Yaounde, is seconded to teach Bafut language in the Catholic's major regional seminary for anglophone Cameroon, and has served as consultant where joint PROPELCA-SIL projects are less successful than his own. Bafut is striking testimony at the local level to the promise for descriptive, socio- and applied linguistics which Tadadjeu in particular saw a decade and more ago, and guided into the channels traced here.[56]

Mundani's and Bafut's achievements have not been replicated in all the indigenous language efforts under PROPELCA and/or SIL auspices. A project began with Limbum, the language of the deeply rural Wimbum people of the North West Province, in 1972. It took six years to form a language committee, overcoming objections from the senior divisional officer (Donga-Mantong) for its "potentially tribalistic" character. Over the next eight years, as the avenues for Mundani and Bafut expression widened, Limbum language efforts faltered because of financial and personal deficiencies. The senior linguist's narrative, dated 1987, described start-and-stop rhythms of publicity and commitment. No "critical mass" of Limbum practitioners developed, so that key personnel could not be replaced if jobs took them elsewhere, and the sponsorship of local churches and PROPELCA did not create significant interest among rural or urban constituencies. Unlike the Mundani case, migrants were not contacted. The publication list lagged behind those connected with other projects of the same longevity. Joseph Mfonyam was brought from Bafut to revitalize the Limbum project, but the pessimistic conclusion to the 1987 report noted that the language committee "has no position of prestige within any governmental or other organization" and raised doubts about its reputation among locals.[57]

Two more examples from anglophone Cameroon will complete this representative profile of current indigenous language prospects in Cameroon. One indicates the difficulties, for it measures both the determination and precariousness of the Ejagham effort to maintain cultural integrity through an indigenous language project. This is a uniquely stressful setting, for the Ejagham are divided by the Nigeria-Cameroon border in a way that places their majority population in

41

the two *divisions* they principally inhabit under the political control of different populations who dominate the capital cities of the *provinces,* the larger political units which contain the Ejagham. The Ejagham find some buffer in their indigenous language publications and a considerable scholarship on the language since 1965. An Ejagham literate described these ventures to the writer in 1989 as his people's "cultural salvation," but a 1985 review of his language disclosed its vulnerable situation. Available and published both technically and popularly in written form since 1970, it claimed just thirty to forty readers and a handful of writers, had no place in any school curriculum, and was spoken for administrative purposes only within the Cameroon political subdivisions inhabited nearly exclusively by the Ejagham. Its future outside libraries and the research domain, as one of the prospective survivors among Tadadjeu's estimate of 100 written and fifty spoken Cameroon languages, is clearly tenuous.[58]

The final example is undocumented in print, but speaks more to the favorable prospects of the entire PROPELCA network as it becomes known, than to the limits perhaps inherent in Ejagham. The writer is aware of a village cluster in North West Province whose urbanized professionals would like its still unwritten Ngie language (long subject to the "dominant vernacular" of Bali in, for instance, printed gospels) to be developed, echoing Mundani initiatives. They place language in the second level among development priorities for a population claimed to be 30,000, next after more schools and a piped water supply. The matrix of language, education, culture and development anticipated here is very much what Tadadjeu's writings and works have sought. Ngie is PROPELCA terrain.[59]

Official Responses to Multilingualism

A survey of governmental reactions to these efforts reveals the national leadership's ambiguity between the constitution's original, unrevised bilingualism and the multilingual experiments documented here. President Ahidjo spoke supportively in 1974 for the research initiatives that preceded Chia's and Tadadjeu's return and PROPELCA. President Biya's tenure since 1982 has yielded some generally positive "signals." He summoned the Association of Cameroonian Poets and Writers to meet in a 1984 colloquium and charged it to survey the broadest possible foundations for Cameroon's cultural identity; and Tadadjeu's first systematic version of "trilingualisme extensif" was delivered to that audience. A similar 1985 colloquium afforded the same opportunity, and the Cameroon Peoples Democratic Movement congress that year passed a resolution favorable to indigenous languages. Again, in 1989, Tadadjeu was invited to give the opening address to the "Etats Généraux" for education, which broke up so tempestuously. His positive reception as Monday's keynote speaker was not compromised by the conference's demise at the week's end.[60]

But there is considerable evidence "on the other hand." The governmental apparatus, as Chumbow wrote in 1980, has neutralized efforts to push the 1961 constitutional formulation more substantially in *any* direction. A linguist with considerable field experience in Cameroon during the 1970s pointed in 1981 to the division of responsibility in the language area between national ministries.[61] The agency (not then advanced to ministerial status) that was the precursor to what is now the Ministry of Higher Education, Computer Services, and Scientific Research organized linguistic research. The Ministry of Education's authority in the public schools controlled the potential experimental classroom settings for multilingual research efforts, but little opportunity was provided to combine the work of researchers and teachers, and classrooms were not made accessible. In fact the original "mission" schools, which the national budget now partially subsidizes, but where curricular and

43

administrative autonomy still persist, have always been more available than state schools in Cameroon to experimental language programs. Outside formal education, the Ministry of Youth and Sports supervised adult literacy (an odd pairing), while the Ministry of Information and Culture managed the artistic and literary production that manifests language use in the most visible and publicly supported channels. Officials from these ministries have seldom coordinated their language strategies, although SIL assembled them for that purpose at a landmark meeting in August 1989.

National Development Plans in the 1980s, one major pulse of government activity, have provided little further guidance. The Ahidjo regime's last version, covering 1981- 1986, contained virtually nothing about linguistic efforts in the chapters devoted to the ministries that shared language jurisdiction. Only one reference to language in any context appeared as a budgetary item, designating CFA 10 million to build an Advanced School of Translators and Interpreters at Buea, to foster and service bilingualism in diplomatic and bureaucratic channels. Nothing in the Plan facilitated indigenous languages.[62]

The next Five Year Plan, Biya's first (for 1986-1991), might have been expected to address multilingualism, given the new president's 1984-1985 initiatives on cultural identity. The Plan's section on the newly created Ministry of Higher Education and Scientific Research included a paragraph on "Linguistic Research."[63] It authorized work on indigenous languages at the level of lexicography, standardization, and socio-linguistic usages. The passage clearly reflected Tadadjeu's interests, but it summarized work already undertaken, indeed largely completed, rather than pushing forward into new program areas, and it was silent about any policy implications the work, and the funds, might entail. The Ministry of Education's section in the text issued in 1986 was as mute on language as that of 1981.

President Biya's own manifesto of 1987, *Communal Liberalism,* continued to mix the bilingual and multilingual signals, although parts of the text on language read as if Tadadjeu himself was the source. It specified exactly the number of Cameroon's spoken and potentially standardized languages that Tadadjeu counted in his 1985 text, and it closely paraphrased his arguments on the horizontal and vertical dimensions of "trilingualisme extensif." As counterweight, however, an earlier passage reverted to Fonlon's emphasis:

> Bilingualism (French and English) should be promoted on a permanent basis in order to ease communication further between Cameroonians of all linguistic backgrounds and to project our country's cultural identity in the world. The two viewpoints are not mutually exclusive, as Tadadjeu has consistently recognized, but resources for their simultaneous implementation are not available. And Biya's text, on the whole, referred often enough to Cameroon's "ethnic particularities," to "sectarianism" and the need for "detribalizing its structures" to lend credence to remarks the writer consistently heard during 1989 about governmental unease that pluralism in language policy could lead to more intensive ethnic fragmentation.[64]

Two recent indications can be cited about the balance of budgetary appropriations and policy tendencies between the bilingual and multilingual activities. As one example, a discretionary part of the presidential budget through the later 1980s funded special bilingual projects designed to promote French and English language parity by giving training and incentives to (perhaps lax or indifferent?) francophones in the public service, including the university, whose English needed work. There is no parallel presidential largesse for indigenous languages.[65]

Another indicator appeared in 1988, when the Ministry of Education issued the first uniform national curriculum guide since Cameroon's independence, for the nursery schools, with the promise that primary and then secondary school curricula would follow (the April 1989 disarray may have compromised this objective for some time ahead). The nursery school document (issued, of course, bilingually) paid considerable attention to the ways the parallel but separate nature of the French and English language domains might be harmonized in a more truly bilingual foundation as four- and five-year-olds learned speech and the rudiments of reading and writing. But there was nothing in the curriculum to indicate a more pluralistic, multilingual language teaching strategy, or any focus at all on indigenous languages as vehicles of instruction or subjects of study. Traditional Cameroon folktales, riddles, songs and other familiar forms of expression for children were the core of the curriculum, and there were concessions inserted like "Limbe Bridge is falling down" when foreign content was used. But every word in the curriculum was rendered in one of the official languages in a guide meant as much for rural area schools as for the cities, which in fact contain most of the nursery schools; all this needs to be considered in light of that age group's highly sensitive and formative language learning phase, which PROPELCA has emphasized. Perhaps the nursery curriculum in the countryside, as taught, is modified by the indigenous speech habits of teachers and students alike, as has happened for generations. Official ministry policy, however, clearly means to standardize these schools to official European language usage.[66]

Fonlon would have welcomed such a strategy, which he devised twenty-five years earlier, had he lived two years longer to see it imprinted, but the now active multilingual cadre can have found less to applaud here. It remains difficult, as Chumbow noted a decade ago, to know what is credited and what is discredited, or indeed what monitor operates between research and policy, rhetoric and action, in the language field. But one has the impression that Fonlon's legacy is like a steamer, on low or no power, drifting on a slack tide, while Tadadjeu's position resembles a canoe, paddled vigorously to create its own current.

It may well be that multilingualism as viewed from "officialdom" is a safe enough research activity, but too contentious for research to be translated into policy and action. Research, yes; implementation, no. The constitution, unchanged since 1961, remains the one common denominator of language policy.

Appraisal and Conclusion

This case study of Cameroon's language policy and practice since independence exemplifies in a wider African context the stress encountered in the search for an effective national strategy that is consonant with the broadest hopes for development. Cameroon's history precludes a monolingual approach; anglophones will not permit a "francophone solution." Although the balance between its indigenous languages is not so different from Tanzania's, no KiSwahili counterpart is available; there are ethnic rivalries, and the more neutral Cameroon Pidgin seems consigned to low prestige despite its expanding use.

The constitution's exogenous bilingualism thus far displays a law of diminishing returns the farther it departs the urban sector, and it divides Cameroonians along lines of class defined by education and office-holding far more than it unites them. Impatience with its effects is predictable beyond the ranks of those engaged in statecraft, bureaucracy, formal education and complex businesses. One cannot discount the genuine tolerance and unity built in leadership circles over thirty years. But assuming some balance between these positive effects and a widespread indifference and cynical impasse which, in their own ways, also "keep the peace" and prevent overt hostility on the language issue, a populace managed and rendered substantially mute by a policy favoring the officially literate elites will not easily generate a productive national development.

The options broadly identified with PROPELCA for multilingualism offer more developmentally sensitive opportunities. They are meant to add value and utility to selected indigenous languages, and join them to the official languages in schools and eventually to Cameroon's working language repertoire. But the opportunities for such pluralism as the multilinguists offer have not yet dislodged the politicians' fears of ethnicity problems, and of course continue to challenge the widely vested, perhaps genuinely "at risk" command of French or English, or both, which establishes current preferences and privileges, not just future opportunities, in

Cameroon.

PROPELCA is experimentally sound in the classrooms and communities it serves, judging from the lengthy report of a Canadian evaluator in 1987. Tadadjeu in 1989, halfway through its projected life span, summarized interim PROPELCA evaluation procedures as follows:

> nos enfants sonts meilleurs que leurs homologues en langue officielle, en calcul et en tout exercice faisant appel à la créativité. Psychologiquement, beaucoup sont fiers d'eux-rnêmes et prennent facilement le risque d'aborder des connaissances nouvelles.[67]

But the project will not be confirmed as a generalized model for language acquisition and use unless widely applied in state schools by the year 2000, while its key practitioners and momentum remain in place.

There are of course, for all these activities, other people besides the linguists who propose and politicians who dispose, whom language interests and affects, and it is now time to address the most striking gap in this study. With the exception of village language committees which have been active in PROPELCA's and SIL's multilingual projects, the focus here has been on the work of language experts and the state apparatus, not the populations in the language communities and their desires. To state the issue directly: neither the constitution's bilingualism thirty years ago nor the subsequent indigenous language initiatives have been held accountable through the franchise or other voluntary expressions of public opinion which would measure enthusiasm, indifference, skepticism or hostility about language policy.

Academic and government debate on language policy has simmered, sometimes flared, for decades, but the writer knows of no widespread recourse to the opinion of the populations affected by the debate, in Cameroon or in Africa at large. The sense of public interests and the force of an informed public have yet to emerge as calculable and accepted dimensions in language policy. Language issues are not as volatile as rice or bread price fluctuations, or import cutbacks. Only in the special conditions of Soweto, 1976, has a language decision created insurrection, although one episode we have recounted here, the Yaounde 1989 education conference which touched Cameroon's language nerve deeply, may have its quiet analogues elsewhere. But there is one most palpable fact of linguistic life: jobs and incomes are by and large correctly perceived as differentially accessible through European language proficiency. French outranks Fe'efe'e as an opportunity structure.

Lacking truly systematic data on the public's views about language policy, brief resort once more to anecdotal evidence may help to address the issue of public consent to Cameroon's indigenous language projects. The story is simple, offered the writer by a school official active and supportive for a decade in Tadadjeu's PROPELCA effort, who told of a protest in Yaounde from parents in a primary school where children participated in an Ewondo language pilot program. Why waste their time and our money on Ewondo, said parents, when the opportunities in Cameroon cluster around competency principally in French, secondarily in English? The minister of education himself, petitioned on the matter, directed the principal of the school that attendance in the Ewondo class should henceforth be voluntary, not to be forced on any child whose family objected.[68]

Several observations occur, in light of this incident. The PROPELCA scheme is both conscientious and contentious. An urban population, articulate beyond the national norm and strategically placed, must be accorded some influence, for it can challenge a perceived threat to personal interests; its elite may wish to consolidate its children's European language edge, its masses may wish to keep the European language aspiration in place for all youths.[69] A well-groomed experiment can lose its grip when a signature or phone call from the top of the policy apparatus intervenes and withdraws that system's support.

This story does not reveal the impacts of PROPELCA's first

49

decade on the relatively anonymous and undifferentiated rural populations. To protest or abandon a PROPELCA classroom would be more difficult in a rural confessional than in an urban state school. This writer's impression, from PROPELCA staff in Yaounde and its sponsors and supporters in anglophone Cameroon outside the capital city, is that the parochial schools which host PROPELCA join the project by virtue of the school authority's decision, informed by parent group consent. It is difficult to determine how "voluntary" the process is, and whether PROPELCA as a school policy variable is independent, for there is a preference for parochial schools over state schools in Cameroon on grounds of test results and discipline, despite the higher costs. Regarding *adult* indigenous language literacy, however, there seems no doubt that rural language committees like Nufi and Mundani's demonstrate popular interest in these initiatives.

We have surveyed Cameroon's language experience, 1960-1990, from many angles. What will it be like in the year 2000? Abandonment of official bilingualism is unlikely. A multilingual policy graft is possible, through expansion of PROPELCA into state schools. But the scheme thus far, for all its multidimensional interests to linguists, has yet to generate the requisite domestic political support and resource allocation.

The final words here, however, must be directed to PROPELCA and Tadadjeu, the catalysts for Cameroon's major language activity for the past decade. It is fair to state that Tadadjeu has attracted attention in recent years which prompts questions in Cameroon about PROPELCA's ultimate objectives, whatever the intent of its original formulation. Since 1981, as we have seen, Tadadjeu has stretched his vocabulary to proclaim indigenous languages not just as resources but as rights to be cultivated by their communities of use, thus raising concerns precisely about ethnic consciousness. And his scholarship has increasingly joined the social philosopher's realm of discourse about development strategy to the linguist's, as he fashions in "African communitarianism" an eloquent critique of étatist sources of thought and action, in favor of a decentralized and pluralistic approach to the resolution of "African crisis" in all its manifestations.[70]

With these views published and his writings reviewed in *Cameroon Tribune,* and as an intellectual prominent enough to have been chosen as opening speaker for the 1989 Etats-Généraux on education, Tadadjeu's voice is recognized and forceful in Cameroon today. To compare his role, though outside government, with Fonlon's a generation ago is appropriate, if we recall Fonlon's departure from government and eventual turn against French after the federal politics prior to 1972 gave way to more unitary structures. It is possible that Tadadjeu's recent writing brings his most fundamental work, PROPELCA, halfway through its projected term, under more scrutiny than it can easily bear in a country with the volatile language politics reflected throughout this study, emphasized by the collapse of the 1989 conference and the minister's dismissal when anglophone- francophone rivalry threatened to ignite. That is not Tadadjeu's struggle, but PROPELCA's agenda for the year 2000 and beyond will stand or fall largely on its capacity to mobilize domestic governmental support and funds. Are the decisions needed to move this agenda likely to favor a scholar turned critic and activist?

By adding these dimensions to his pioneer work clustering descriptive, socio- and applied linguistics, Tadadjeu tests the confines of the "comfort zone" for debate about Cameroon's national unity in the context of its pluralism. It will be unfortunate if Tadadjeu's work as a linguist is compromised by the additions to his repertoire. More is surely to be heard from and about PROPELCA and Tadadjeu in the next decade. The discourse will be instructive about both the place of indigenous languages in Cameroon and the linguist's role, and their limits. It will continue to reflect the tension in Cameroon between the exigencies of a cautious statecraft and the search for alternative policies in language, education and culture, and their bearings on the unresolved debate, common throughout Africa, about national development strategy.

51

End Notes

Generous assistance is acknowledged throughout these notes, but I must first record the continuous support and courtesy of Dr. Paul Nkwi before and throughout the period of seven months in Cameroon, 1989, when this paper took shape.

[1] For the lack of case law, see C. Anyangwe, "The Legal Aspect of Bilingualism," *Revue Science et Technique,* Serie Sciences Humaines III, 3-4 (1985), pp. 5-14.

[2] There is debate about the number of Cameroon's indigenous languages. P. Alexandre, *Languages and Language in Black Africa* (Evanston: Northwestern University, 1972), p. 90, and E. Chia, "Cameroon Home Languages," in E. Koenig, E. Chia and J. Povey (eds.), *A Sociolinguistic Profile of Urban Centers in Cameroon* (Los Angeles: Crossroads Press, 1983), p. 19, discern roughly 100. But the most recent scholarly usage, which Cameroon's official documents echo, favors the larger number. See Conference des Ministres de l'Education des Etats d'Expression Francaise (CONFEMEN), *Promotion et Integration des Langues Nationales dans les Systemes Educatifs: Bilan et Inventaire* (paris: Champion, 1986), p. 90; M. Mann and D. Dalby, *A Thesaurus of African Languages* (London; K.G. Saur, 1987), pp. 180-181; the work of Maurice Tadadjeu used in the second part of this paper. I adopt the larger number here, recognizing the problems inherent in the vocabulary of "language" and "dialect," intercomprehension, etc.

[3] Among the few anglophone sources in the general literature which have noticed the work considered here is B. Weinstein, "Language Planning in Francophone Africa," *Language Problems and Language Planning* 4, 1 (1980), pp. 66-67. See CONFEMEN, *Promotion et Integration.* for recognition of Cameroon in more detailed, specialist sources.

[4] The need in 1960-1961 to bring French and British trust territories together pre-empted a monolingual approach in Cameroon, and it needs no direct analysis here. But there have been regrets about that situation and occasional efforts to redress it. Those so persuaded, mainly francophones, cite the familiar "one language, one state" and "all quiet on the language front" monolingual resolutions of pluralist language disputes. From this standpoint, what Fishman calls the "nationist" priority, and the orthodox measures derived from Karl Deutsch's approach assessing national cohesion by the ease with which (for example) economic transactions and communications links are established, are what matter. For Fishman's formulation of nationism, see J. Fishman, "Nationality-Nationalism and Nation-Nationism," in J. Fishman, C. Ferguson, and J. Das Gupta (eds.), *Language Problems of Developing Nations* (New York: John Wiley, 1968), pp. 39-51. For Deutsch, see K. Deutsch, *Nationalism and Social Communication: An Enquiry into the Foundations of Nationality* 2nd ed. (Cambridge, MA: MIT, 1966). For Fishman on Deutsch and the ramifications of his approach, see J. Fishman et. al., *The Rise and Fall of the Ethnic Revival* (Berlin: Mouton, 1985), pp. 496 ff.

[5] The still earlier context is the Phelps-Stokes literature of the 1920s, but UNESCO, *The Use of Vernacular Languages in Education* (Paris, 1953), the published proceedings of the 1951 meeting, is the fundamental source for modern policy debate. The word *indigenous* is used in most cases below, instead of local, vernacular or national, in order to avoid the confusion that the third of those alternatives in particular can lead to in a discussion which is not meant to be highly technical.

[6] Fishman, *Rise and Fall,* p. 470.

[7] The newspaper, typically for the one-party state situation that prevailed in 1989, took its direction from the government's appointments to its management staff. A handful of independent weeklies supplemented the Tribune, none very critically in a climate where closure for "irresponsible journalism" was a threat; see n. 10 below. A more varied and critical press has since emerged alongside Cameroon Tribune, reflecting a cautiously more pluralistic politics.

[8] C. Geary, *On Legal Change in Cameroon: Women, Marriage and Bridewealth*. Boston University African Studies Center, Working Paper #113 (1986), pp. 20-29.

[9] *Ibid.*, p. 29. See p. 25 for commentary on how Pidgin is perceived to compromise its users: "I have not yet met any well-educated Anglophone Cameroonian who does not know how to speak and understand Pidgin. However, it is common that for reasons of status people deny their knowledge of this"bastard" language as some call it."

[10] *Cameroon Tribune* coverage was perfunctory, simply recording a ministerial shuffle. The mid-May issue of the independent local journal *Hebdo* (12-18 May, p. 2) noted the episode and the surprise of Ngango's dismissal without a word about the reasons. The Cameroon public's first substantial access to the story may have been the September 1989 edition of the imported magazine *New African* under the caption, p. 39, "Ngango falls from grace to grass." This writer unsuccessfully sought entry to the assembly, but during that and subsequent weeks interviewed six delegates or observers about its conduct and aftermath. This account is reconstructed from those interviews.

[11] This particular sense of grievance for anglophone against francophone surfaces periodically and dramatically in more public places than the Palais, and needs to be raised in preparation for the materials on language which follow, especially as it touches bilingualism. A mimeographed "Open Letter To All English-Speaking Parents of Cameroon," issued 20 August 1985, covered eight pages with language such as "Tell us why bilingualism ... demands the mastery of the French language by Anglophones and not vice versa," and raised issues across a range of disproportionality including scholarships abroad, radio, road, harbor and power station facilities. "Harmonization," p. 3, was attacked in precisely the way manifested at the Palais in 1989. On 26 May 1990, more publicized than anything recounted in this study, an encounter with police after an inaugural rally in anglophone Bamenda for a Social Democratic

Front alternative political party left six people dead, in circumstances not yet fully determined. A recent comprehensive study of Cameroon frames issues treated here by reference to "very great potential for conflict and the formation of a nationalism around some form of anglophone identity, and even separatism or a desire for separate independence ... this potential has plagued Cameroon's independence history"; M. DeLancey, *Cameroon: Dependence and Independence* (Boulder: Westview, 1989), p. 99.

[12] H. Rudin, *Germans in the Cameroons,* 1884-1914: *A Case Study in Modern Imperialism* (New Haven: Yale University, 1938), pp. 353-360, remains useful.

[13] R. Stumpf, *La Politique Linguistique au Cameroun de* 1884 à *1960* (Berne: Peter Lang, 1979), especially pp. 80-82, 103-104 on uniformity of purpose despite mission and (later) United Nations agency influences working for indigenous language elbow room. For colonial French Africa at large, on assimilative language use in schools and the resultant culture, see G. Kelly, "Learning to be Marginal: Schooling in Interwar French Africa," *Journal of Asian and African Studies* XXI, 3/4 (1986), pp. 171-184. Weinstein, cited in n. 3 above, surveyed the post-colonial pressure to maintain French in Africa. Cameroon's leading advocate of multilingualism, the key voice later in this study, noted in 1989 that indigenous languages now convey early formal education throughout the world, with the notable exception of francophone Black Africa: M. Tadadjeu on p. 1 of his speech opening Yaounde's Etats-Généraux, "La Problématique des Langues Nationales dans le Contexte de la Réforme du Système Educatif Camerounais," (1989).

[14] V. Amaazie, "The 'Igbo Scare' in the British Cameroons, c. 1945-1961," *Journal of African History* 31 (1990), pp. 281-293, traces the preference by 1960 for linkage to the east because of grievances with the most influential Nigerians in West Cameroon.

[15] W. Johnson, *The Cameroon Federation: Political Integration in a Fragmented Society* (Princeton: Princeton University, 1970), pp. 300 ff. surveys the nation's education during the 1960s. G. Courade and C.

Courade, *L'Ecole du Cameroun Anglophone* (Yaounde: ONAREST, 1977) is the ranking source for West Cameroon, based on its government's key document, *West Cameroon Education Policy: Investment in Education* (Buea, 1963), its implementation and consequences.

[16] Johnson, *Cameroon Federation,* pp. 291-316 remains the most accessible source for Fonlon until 1970, and this survey supplements his to that year (although, in my reading, p. 297 overemphasizes the role Fonlon gave African languages *in schools).* I draw for Fonlon after 1970 on his later publications, on N. Lyonga (ed.), *Socrates in Cameroon: The Life and Works of Bernard Nsokika Fonlon* (Yaounde and Leeds: Tortoise Books, 1989), and on the generosity in 1989 of Drs. Nalova Lyonga and Innocent Foucha in Yaounde and Patrick Mbunwe-Samba in Bamenda, who provided copies of Fonlon's unpublished writings and details about his later years.

[17] B. Fonlon, "A Case for Early Bilingualism," *Abbia* 4 (1963), pp. 62-64.

[18] *Ibid.,* pp. 66-69. His deepest loyalty as against his policy conviction can be gauged from a remark in an unpublished paper, "Education through Literature" (1977), p. 35: "I do not worship English. I worship Lamnso." This was his mother tongue.

[19] Fonlon, "A Case," pp. 67-71.

[20] *Ibid.,* pp. 87-88.

[21] *Ibid,* pp. 91-94.

[22] Koenig, *Sociolinguistic Profiles,* An empirically rich source, the volume yields more impressionistic than statistically firm results because its six essays, though introduced by a "profile" of Cameroon's language usage, were not concluded by any definitive coordination of their findings. It nonetheless reveals multilingual use patterns not just holding but expanding in the face of bilingual policy.

[23] *Ibid.,* pp. 94, 96, 111.

[24] *Ibid.,* pp. 15-17, 52, 55. Various portions of the volume disclosed the growing use of Cameroon Pidgin, and its intrusion on speedy and accurate learning of standard English, acquired less easily than French because of Pidgin's "watering down" effect in anglophone sections; this partly explains the prejudice found above in Wum and in learned and official anglophone circles generally, where defense of standard English has a rationale on both domestic political and international educational access grounds.

[25] W. Ekane, "The Effects of Bilingual Education in Cameroon: A Follow Up Study of the Bilingual Grammar School Graduates, Buea, Cameroon" (Ed.D. Dissertation, Syracuse University, 1988), p. 94.

[26] 400 were both questionnaire respondents and were interviewed, the remainder only answered the questionnaires.

[27] *Ibid.,* pp. 180-184 for the presentation of positive BGS results, pp. 175, 211, 227 for shortcomings, pp. 218-233 for general assessment.

[28] *Ibid.,* p. 57.

[29] B. Chumbow, "Language and Language Policy in Cameroon," in N. Kofele-Kale (ed.), *An African Experiment in Nation Building; the Bilingual Cameroon Republic Since Reunification* (Boulder: Westview, 1980), pp. 281-316.

[30] *Ibid.,* pp. 288-289; emphasis is original.

[31] *Ibid.,* p. 297.

[32] G. Tchoungui, "Focus on Official Bilingualism in Cameroon: Its Relationship to Education," in Koenig, *Sociolinguistic Profile,* p. 113.

[33] *Ibid.,* p 114.

[34] B. Fonlon, "To Every African Freshman: Ten Years After," *Abbia* 34-37 (1979), pp. 48-52, committing to print what he had spoken and written since 1977. Anglophone interests were always an element in

57

his bilingualism, though the visionary outweighed the pragmatist; see Johnson, *Cameroon Federation,* pp. 294-95.

[35] J. Kisob, "A Live Language: 'Pidgin English'," *Abbia* 1 (1963), pp. 25-31. Current advocates among anglophones, against the grain of the Wum evidence above, stress Pidgin's practical benefits. Dr. Kevin Gumne, who organizes rural education in the Bamenda area, is exemplary.

[36] Ngijol, "Nécessité d'une langue nationale," *Abbia* 7 (1964), pp. 83-99, admitting the need for considerable time, money, and developmental effort before any Cameroon language would be serviceable. The Ewondo reference, p. 95, slipped in late, but must have raised dust. P. Ngijol, *Etude sur l'enseignement des langues et cultures nationales* (Yaounde: Centre National de l'Education, 1978) proposed support for six national languages. I am grateful for the information about Ngijol's abandonment in 1989 of the 1964 approach, while speaking at a Yaounde seminar, and for assistance throughout my work, to Elisabeth Gfeller of Société Internationale de Linguistique.

[37] I wish to acknowledge their generous assistance during 1989 as the following material was assembled. Tadadjeu in particular provided unpublished papers and made time for invaluable discussions. Their work described here is clearly aligned with similar African projects they encountered in the 1970s, such as the Yoruba Six Year Primary Project, and keeps as current as African conditions permit with later projects like that documented in P. Kokora, *Le Projet d'Education Préscolaire en Langue Maternelle en Côte d'Ivoire.* Boston University African Studies Center. Issues in Language and Education #3 (1990), which Tadadjeu has visited.

[38] These two early sources are M. Tadadjeu, "Language Planning in Cameroon: Toward a Trilingual Education System," in R. Herbert (ed.), *Patterns in Language. Culture and Society: Sub-Saharan Africa,* Ohio State University Working Papers in Linguistics 19 (1975), pp. 53-75, and M. Tadadjeu, "Cost-Benefit Analysis and Language Education Planning in Sub-Saharan Africa," in P. Kotey and H. Der-Houssikian

(eds.), *Language and Linguistic Problems in Africa* (Columbia, SC: Hornbeam Press, 1977), pp. 3-33.

[39] The strategy emerged in papers locally circulated before its most accessible formulation in M. Tadadjeu, "Le facteur linguistique du projet social camerounais," *Journal of West African Languages* XVIII (1987), pp. 23-34.

[40] The 1981 text was Tadadjeu's unsigned contribution "Les Langues," *L'Encyclopédie de La République Unie du Cameroun*. I (Abidjan: New African Publications, 1981), pp. 261-87, which is the source for these criteria, later elaborated in unpublished papers.

[41] Tadadjeu, "Language Planning," p. 68; emphasis is original.
[42] This and the preceding paragraph are drawn principally from Tadadjeu, "Language Planning," pp. 68-69, and two later publications: M. Tadadjeu and E. Chia, "Projet de Recherche Opérationelle pour l'Enseignement des Langues au Cameroun (PROPELCA)," in M. Tadadjeu and E. Sadembouo (eds.), *Recherche en Langues et Linguistique au Cameroun* (Yaounde: DGRST 1982), pp. 21-33; M. Tadadjeu, E. Gfeller, and G. Mba, *Manuel de Formation pour l' enseignement des langues nationales dans les écoles primaires* (Universite de Yaounde, 1988), esp. pp. 29-64. For German and French, see Tadadjeu, "Language Planning," p. 60; "Les Langues" p. 271; and M. Tadadjeu, "For a Policy of Cameroonian Linguistic Integration: Extensive Trilingualisrn," in Cameroon. Ministry of Information and Culture. *The Cultural Identity of Cameroon* (Yaounde, 1985), p. 189. The contrast with Fonlon on the classics is clear. Tadadjeu told the writer (3 July 1989) that those supporting German and Spanish, still taught and tested in francophone Cameroon, would like them spread to the anglophone region, and that Greek and Latin advocates are working to expand the classical language curriculum.

[43] The French quotations from 1981 in "Les Langues," pp. 275-76 are precise renditions of Tadadjeu's convictions elaborated more generally in the next few years.

[44] For these numbers see Tadadjeu, "For a policy," p. 179, Tadadjeu et. al., *Manuel de Formation,* p. 53, and a recent paper he supervised: L. Dunnigan, "Mother Tongue Literacy in Cameroon: A Language Planning Perspective," A Mémoire for the Degree of Maîtrise in Linguistics, University of Yaounde (1989) pp. 24, 28, a valuable source for this and other particulars which I very much appreciate the author's permission to read and cite. Chia, as cited in n. 2, in 1983 counted 93 and estimated a maximum of 120 indigenous languages.

[45] Tadadjeu, "For a policy," p. 180.

[46] Tadadjeu, "Cost-Benefit Analysis," p. 7.

[47] This paragraph and the next rely on the sources cited above, n. 39, interviews and site observations.

[48] The network, in fact, takes up slack that PROPELCA's funding limits create, and the cumulative effect of indigenous language activity is greater than strict accountancy shows. For an independent review of the network, see CONFEMEN, *Promotion et Intégration,* pp. 92-94, 101-105, which data challenge Tchoungui's most trenchant criticism, noted above.

[49] *Bibliography of the Work of SIL in Cameroon up till August* 1988; P. Baer, "Computer Technology and Cameroon Languages," *Revue Science et Technique,* Serie Sciences Humaines II, 1/2 (1984), pp. 29-44. One is naturally curious about the precise nature of the Cameroon-SIL agreements, but I did not pursue the issue. SIL's and PROPELCA's interests overlap; they need and use each other's resources, as the example of Joseph Mfonyam below indicates. From my observations, any tensions between foreign evangelical and indigenous scholarly policy and motivations are tacitly restrained.

[50] CONFEMEN, *Promotion et Intégration,* p. 7. S. Hoben, *Language and Education Reform in Rwanda.* Boston University African Studies Center. Issues in Language and Education #2 (1988), recorded a turn to the indigenous language as sole medium of primary school instruction. She found practical and psychological advantages in the spread of its

domain, but diminished competence in other languages. The experiment's outcome in her view "is still an open question," p. 15. Cameroon and PROPELCA are not parallel cases.

[51] The first Fe'efe'e efforts date from 1928 and the French priest Father Gontier, but encountered resistance at the same time that Mandate officials suppressed the far better known efforts by Sultan Njoya at Foumban to continue his work on a written form of Bamoun (or Bamum). Bamileke themselves resumed the Fe'efe'e project twenty-five years later. See Cameroon, Ministère de I'Education Nationale, *Bullétin d'information de la commission nationale pour I' UNESCO* #21 (Yaounde, 1973); Agence de coopération culturelle et technique, *Promotion des Langues Nationales: Résultats des Travaux* (Yaounde, 1976); E. Sadembouo and J. Watters, *A Proposal for Determining the Development Levels of a Written Language* (Yaounde, 1985), pp. 16-26; CONFEMEN, *Promotion et Intégration*, pp. 95-96.

[52] Tadadjeu, "Language Planning," p. 59, and "Les Langues," p. 272.

[53] The major source here is the SIL linguist's report, M. Annett, "Exploring Urban Mother Tongue Literacy,"*Journal of West African Languages* XVII, 1 (1987), pp. 60-73, supplemented by SIL's house publications and in 1989 by *Cameroon Tribune* accounts of the appearance of a Mundani Gospel of Luke.

[54] Ibid., p. 69; emphasis is original.

[55] J. Watters, "L'alphabétisation en langues nationales: mythe ou réalité: Etude de cas," *Actes du séminaire régionale UNESCO-CONFEJES pour L'Afrique centrale* (Yaounde, 1987), p.163.

[56] Evidence for Bafut is widely distributed in PROPELCA and SIL sources. I am particularly indebted to Dr. Mfonyam for lengthy talks and his hospitality on site visits in Bafut which augment this paragraph's detail.

[57] V. Bradley, *The Development and Activities of a Language Committee-the Wimbum Literacy Association,* (Yaounde: SIL, 1986), p. 14 for the quotation.

[58] Here, conversation with Peter Tambe-Nchinge supplements SIL evidence, principally Sadembouo and Watters, *ap. cit.,* pp. 26-31. All this sharply contrasts with the account of a vigorous ideographic writing tradition among the Ejagham, still persisting in the homeland aesthetic and in Cuba, in R. Thompson, *Flash of the Spirit* (New York: Vintage, 1984), Ch. 5.

[59] Walter Agharih, a veterinarian, and Richard Ubangoh, a seismologist, are the Ngie sources. Attentive readers will have noted the absence of northern Cameroon on these pages. SIL's evangelism carries five of its twenty-three programs to the Muslim north (past Garoua), but PROPELCA has not ventured north and this study therefore stays south.

[60] Tadadjeu reviewed the favorable signals in "Le facteur linguistique," pp. 27-30.

[61] C. Fluckiger, "Language Planning in the Heart of Linguistic Complexity" (unpublished ms., 1981), p. 5.

[62] Cameroon Ministry of Economic Affairs and Planning, *The Fifth Five-Year Economic, Social and Cultural Development Plan.* 1981-1986 (Yaounde, 1981), pp. 245-54,281-85,309-34; p. 334 designated the funds for ASTI which, in conjunction with the nearby Bilingual Grammar School, make Buea the official language hub.

[63] Cameroon Ministry of the Plan and Regional Development, *Sixth Five-Year Economic. Social and Cultural Development Plan.* 1986-1991 (Yaounde, 1986), p. 264.

[64] P. Biya, *Communal Liberalism* (London: Macmillan, 1987), pp. 104-105 for the echoes of Tadadjeu, p. 34 for the support of bilingualism, pp. 31, 34, 44 for references to the dangers of fragmentation.

[65] I thank Ann Rossiter and Simon Hill, the British Council specialists operating these programs until mid-1989, for time and materials which familiarized me with these ambitious, well equipped projects,

funded jointly by Great Britain and Cameroon under authority of Decree No. 85-1200, *Official Gazette of the Republic of Cameroon,* 15 September 1985.

[66] Cameroon Ministry of National Education, *Cameroon Nursery Education Syllabus* (Yaounde, 1988).

[67] Tadadjeu, "La Problématique," p. 18, from his Palais speech. This appraisal, closely resembling the Yoruba experimental results, summarized the evaluation report submitted in 1987 to the Canadian Agency for International Development, a major PROPELCA funding source; J. Cairns, "Experimental Mother Tongue Literacy Program, Cameroon: Final Evaluation" (1987).

[68] William Banboye, director of Catholic education in the Bamenda area, is the source.

[69] See Weinstein, *Language Planning.* pp. 72-74, for acute judgment a decade ago about cases like this one from Yaounde, the competing interests engaged in all African language arenas, and the potential crisis of legitimacy for states which play them off and defer clear decisions.

[70] Thus a major recent publication, M. Tadadjeu, *Voie Africaine: Esquisse du Communautarisme Africain* (Yaounde: Club OAU, 1989), and his new periodical venture since May 1989, *Afrique Unie: Revue Semestrielle Interdisciplinaire.* Conversations with Drs. Marcien Towa and Orner Yembe about these issues helped frame this appraisal.

Bibliography

Afrique Unie: Revue Semestrielle Interdisciplinaire 1,1 (1989).

Agence de coopération culturelle et technique, Promotion des Langues Nationales: Résultats des Travaux (Yaounde, 1976).

P. Alexandre, *Languages and Language in Black Africa* (Evanston: Northwestern University, 1972).

V. Amaazee, "The 'Igbo Scare' in the British Cameroons, c.1945-61," *Journal of African History* 31 (1990), pp. 281-293.

M. Annett, "Exploring Urban Mother Tongue Literacy," *Journal of West African Languages* XVII,1 (1987), pp. 60-73.

C. Anyangwe, "The Legal Aspect of Bilingualism," *Revue Science et Technique,* Série Sciences Humaines III,3-4 (1985), pp. 5-14.

P. Baer, "Computer Technology and Cameroon Languages," *Revue Science et Technique,* Série Sciences Humaines II,1/2 (1984), pp. 29-44.

P. Biya, *Communal Liberalism* (London: Macmillan, 1987).

V. Bradley, *The Development and Activities of a Language Committee - the Wimbum Literacy Association* (Yaounde: SIL, 1986).

J. Cairns, "Experimental Mother Tongue Literacy Program, Cameroon: Final Evaluation" (1987).

Cameroon. Ministère de l'Education Nationale. *Bulletin d'information de la commission nationale pour l'UNESCO* #21 (Yaounde, 1973).

_____ . Ministry of Economic Affairs and Planning. *The Fifth Five-Year Economic, Social and Cultural Development Plan, 1981-1986* (Yaounde, 1981).

_____ . Decree No. 85-1200. *Official Gazette of the Republic of Cameroon, 15* September 1985.

_____ . Ministry of the Plan and Regional Development. *Sixth Five-Year Economic, Social and Cultural Plan,* 1986-1991 (Yaounde, 1986).

_____ . Ministry of National Education. *Cameroon Nursery Education Syllabus* (Yaounde, 1988).

E. Chia, "Cameroon Home Languages," in E. Koenig, E. Chia and J. Povey (eds.), *A Sociolinguistic Profile of Urban Centers in Cameroon* (Los Angeles: Crossroads Press, 1983), pp.19-32.

B. Chumbow, "Language and Language Policy in Cameroon," in N. Kofele-Kale (ed.), *An African Experiment in Nation Building: The Bilingual Cameroon Republic Since Reunification* (Boulder: Westview Press, 1980), pp. 281-323.

Conférence des Ministres de l'Education des Etats d'Expression Francaise (CONFEMEN), *Promotion et Intégration des Langues Nationales dans les Systèmes Educatifs: Bilan et Inventaire* (Paris: Champion, 1986).

G. Courade and C. Courade, *L'Ecole du Cameroun Anglophone* (Yaounde: ONAREST, 1977).

M. Delancey, *Cameroon: Dependence and Independence* (Boulder: Westview, 1989).

K. Deutsch, *Nationalism and Social Communication: An Enquiry into the Foundations of Nationality* 2nd ed. (Cambridge: MIT, 1966).

L. Dunnigan, "Mother Tongue Literacy in Cameroon: A Language Planning Perspective," Mémoire for the Degree of Maîtrise in Linguistics, University of Yaounde (1989).

C. Eastman, *Language Planning: An Introduction* (San Francisco: Chandler and Sharp, (1983).

W. Ekane, "The Effects of Bilingual Education: A Follow up Study of the Bilingual Grammar School (BGS) Graduates, Buea Cameroon," Ed.D. Dissertation, Syracuse University (1988).

J. Fishman, "Nationality-Nationalism and Nation-Nationism," in J. Fishman, C. Ferguson and J. Das Gupta (eds.), *Language Problems of Developing Nations* (New York: John Wiley, 1968), pp. 39-51.

_____ et. al., *The Rise and Fall of the Ethnic Revival* (Berlin: Mouton, 1985).

C. Fluckiger, "Language Planning in the Heart of Linguistic Complexity" (unpublished ms., 1981).

B. Fonlon, "A Case for Early Bilingualism," *Abbia* 4 (1963), pp. 56-94.

_____ , "Education through Literature" (unpublished ms., 1977).

_____ , " To Every African Freshman: Ten Years After," *Abbia* 34-37 (1979), pp. 9-55.

C. Geary, *On Legal Change in Cameroon: Women, Marriage and Bridewealth.*

Boston University African Studies Center, Working Paper #113 (1986).

K. Gumne and P. Mzeka, *The Role of Pidgin English in Communicating Rural Development in Cameroon* (Buea, 1989).

S. Hoben, *Language and Education Reform in Rwanda*. Boston University African Studies Center. Issues in Language and Education #3 (1988).

W. Johnson, *The Cameroon Federation: Political Integration in a Fragmented Society* (Princeton: Princeton University, 1970).

G. Kelly, "Learning to be Marginal: Schooling in Interwar French Africa," *Journal of Asian and African Studies* XXXI, 3/4 (1986), pp. 171-184.

J. Kisob, "A Live Language: 'Pidgin English'," *Abbia* 1 (1963), pp.25-31.

E. Koenig, E.Chia and J. Povey (eds.), *A Sociolinguistic Profile of Urban Centers in Cameroon* (Los Angeles: Crossroads Press, 1983).

P. Kokora, *Le Projet d'Education Préscolaire en Langue Maternelle en Côte d'Ivoire*. Boston University African Studies Center. Issues in Language and Education #5 (1990).

N. Lyonga (ed.), *Socrates in Cameroon: The Life and Works of Bernard Nsokika Fonlon* (Yaounde and Leeds: Tortoise Books, 1989).

M. Mann and D.Dalby, *A Thesaurus of African Languages* (London: K.G. Saur, 1987).

P. Ngijol, "Nécessité d'une langue nationale," *Abbia* 7 (1964), pp. 83-99.

———, *Etude sur l'enseignement des langues et cultures nationals* (Yaounde: Centre National de L'Education, 1978).

Open Letter to All English-Speaking parents of Cameroon from the English-Speaking Students of the North-West and South-West Provinces (1985).

C. Robinson, "The Place of Local-Language Literacy in Rural Development in Cameroon: Presentation of an Experimental Program," *African Studies Review* 33, 3 (1990), pp. 53-64.

H. Rudin, *Germans in the Cameroons, 1884-1914: A Case Study in Modern Imperialism* (New Haven: Yale University, 1938).

E. Sadembouo and J. Watters, *A Proposal for Determining the Development*

Levels of a Written Language (Yaounde, 1985).

Société Internationale de Linguistique, Cameroon. *Annual Report*, 1987-1988.

_____ . *Bibliography of SIL in Cameroon up till August 1988*.

R. Stumpf, *La Politique Linguistique au Cameroon de* 1884 à *1960* (Berne: Peter Lang, 1979).

M. Tadadjeu, "Language Planning in Cameroon: Toward a Trilingual Education System," in R. Herbert (ed.), *Patterns in Language, Culture and Society: Sub-Saharan Africa*. Ohio State University Working Papers in Linguistics 19 (1975), pp. 53-75.

_____ , "Cost-Benefit Analysis and Language Education Planning in Sub-Saharan Africa," in P. Kotey and H. Der-Houssikian (eds.), *Language and Linguistic Problems in Africa* (Columbia, S.C.: Hornbeam Press, 1977), pp. 3-33.

_____ , "Les Langues," in *L'Encyclopédie de la République Unie du Cameroun* Tome 1 (Abidjan: New African Publications, 1981), pp. 261-287.

_____ , "For a Policy of Cameroonian Linguistic Integration: Extensive Trilingualisme," in Cameroon, Ministry of Information and Culture. *The Cultural Identity of Cameroon* (Yaounde, 1985), pp. 178-192.

_____ , "Le facteur linguistique du projet social camerounais," *Journal of West African Languages* XVII,1 (1987), pp. 23-34.

_____ , "Le Problématique des Langues Nationales dans le contexte de la Reforme du Systèrne Educatif Camerounais" (1989).

_____ , *Voie Africaine: Esquisse du Communautarisme Africain* (Yaounde: Club OAU, 1989).

_____ , and E. Chia, "Projet de Recherche Opérationelle pour l'Enseignement des Langues au Cameroun (PROPELCA)," in M. Tadadjeu and E. Sadembou (eds.), *Recherche en Langues et Linguistique au Cameroun* (Yaounde: DGRST, 1982), pp. 21-33.

_____ , E. Gfeller, and G. Mba, *Manuel de Formation pour l'enseignement des langues nationales dans les écoles primaires* (Yaounde: PROPELCA, 1988).

G. Tchoungui, "Focus on Official Bilingualism in Cameroon: Its

67

Relationship to Education," in E. Koenig, E. Chia and J. Povey (eds.), *A Sociolinguistic Profile of Urban Centers in Cameroon* (Los Angeles: Crossroads Press, 1983), pp. 93-115.

R. Thompson, *Flash of the Spirit* (New York: Vintage, 1984).

UNESCO. *The Use of Vernacular Languages in Education* (Paris, 1953).

H. Vernon-Jackson, *Language, Schools and Government in Cameroon* (New York: Teachers College,
1967).

J. Watters, "L'alphabétisation en langues nationales: mythe ou réalité. Etude de cas," *Actes du séminaire régionale UNESCO-CONFEJES pour l'Afrique centrale* (Yaounde, 1987), pp.153-165.

B. Weinstein, "Language Planning in Francophone Africa," *Language Problems and Language Planning* 4, (1980), pp. 55-77.

The government's unease about what was at stake in this field of enquiry associated with Tadadjeu turned out to be even more delicate than I'd anticipated, which should (in 2013 retrospect) have been reinforced, but was not, by the 1985 Open Letter's first circulation in formal print in 1990, after my departure from Cameroon but before my own text's 1991 publication. 1985's text surfaced in a 1990 anthology edited and published by a ranking dissident of his generation with nearly a decade's experience in Cameroon jails, the anglophone Albert Mukong. Entitled *The Case for the Southern Cameroons*, his book was the first prominent manifesto from an anglophone movement sustained for a generation since then and (still, a decade after Mukong's death in 2004) pressing beyond a revival of federalism and a Québec-like autonomy into the Southern Cameroons National Council's call for secession and independence. Not just scholarly or theoretical in nature and interest, language was a Cameroon governance concern and a symptom of larger disorders, increasingly so during my 1990s in-country research and then as my writing continued past 2000.

If I did not anticipate Mukong's 1990 publication's later significance in my 1989 research leading to 1991's text, I did understand and note (on 1991's last page) that Cameroon's efforts fell short of Tadadjeu's <u>own</u> aspirations and agenda, judging by his substantial book, transcending linguistic issues and experiments, decidedly pan-African and incipiently critical, published in 1989 by Club OAU in Yaounde, *Voie Africaine: Esquisse du Communautarisme Africain* (I would like to know more than I do about Tadadjeu's role as a CPDM member in the National Assembly a few years later). In any event, on ever more obvious policy and politics grounds, consonant with but perhaps more intensely than for routine Africa-wide statecraft ca. 1990, public sector reticence rather than innovation caught my attention in the fields of study my early Cameroon research and writing explored.

PROPELCA-SIL collaboration continues to this day, although (because of my abrupt scholarly shift described below, Chapter 3) I do not know if additional programs have been fielded beyond those operating in 1990, if longitudinal research is available for later or current evaluation of the local programs, or if Cameroon government funding for PROPELCA was renewed past the original commitment through 2000. Scanning SIL's 2013 on-line publications list for Cameroon while preparing this book, I found well past 2,000 entries, ranging from gospel texts through, in SIL's terms, PROPELCA's smaller scale subsidiary productions; anyone interested in pursuing this story can do so through this SIL source.

There is a further sequel to report. Tadadjeu died 30 December 2012, as I began to write this commentary for the present volume. He had prepared, just after we last met in 1989, a paper I knew nothing about at the time, presented in Washington, D.C., 1990. It was published by SIL International in 2004, and closely aligned Tadadjeu's and my own perspectives on the culture-education-language-development matrix. Tadadjeu's 1990 abstract, unchanged for 2004, noted that development policy over three decades using non-African models "has resulted in regression" but (referring to PROPELCA) that "several years of successful educational experimentation in mother tongues in Cameroon" offered better development options. The body of this "Language, Literacy and Education in African Development: A Perspective from Cameroon" paper, easily accessible electronically through SIL sourcing, provides anyone interested in Tadadjeu's applied scholarship legacy his own definitive statement, and a companion to and check on my own interpretive work appearing here.

There were critiques of Tadadjeu's efforts. H. Russell Bernard, as I prepared this text in 2013, alerted me to experimental research he and colleagues carried out at Njinikom, North West Province just after my 1989 time in Cameroon. It questioned PROPELCA for overly complex orthographic usage based on external methods and standards, and the consequent delay in the spread of "popular literacy" when time for language preservation, including Njinikom's own, was growing short. But Tadadjeu's career accomplishments register in the International Linguapax Award conferred by a Spanish foundation on International Mother Language Day, 2005, recognition accorded Joshua Fishman and Neville Alexander among others who advocate and work for the "article of faith" objective, in policy and principle, of maintaining global linguistic diversity.

The legacy of his entire body of work also registers in a cognate news item, in process since 1978 and still playing out 8,000 miles from Cameroon but just 80 miles from my own home, made prominent the very week of Tadadjeu's obsequies in Yaounde and his native Dschang. My area's major daily newspaper, *The Seattle Times* (23 January 2013), printed Lynda Mapes' story on the almost extinct "mother tongue" Klallam (Native American, Salishan) language's revival and recovery at the remote northwest corner of Washington state (U.S.A.). Linguist Timothy Montler began the study of Klallam in 1978 when only 100 speakers remained among 5,000 in the community. That number dwindled to just two by 2012. In the interval, however, thirty-eight Klallam people compiled words and recounted stories that Montler's scholarly team turned from orality into a 12,000 word dictionary published late in 2012. By this time a community project (resembling PROPELCA-SIL efforts) also offered Klallam language, history and culture as "content material" in its schools, while the region's largest secondary school, some distance from Klallam soil, offered Klallam alongside French and Spanish for graduation credit.

This would surely have pleased Tadadjeu, as it would his surviving Cameroonian colleagues and those new in the field.

Chapter 2

Abbia and culture's chasms

Bamenda was the primary site for my second project begun in 1989, the first systematic scholarship published on *Abbia: Cameroon Cultural Review*, a journal with forty numbers issued over twenty years, 1963-1982, appearing more frequently early than late in its life. Although this analysis was not published until 1996, and a paper dated 1994 is reprinted here in Chapter 3 following 1996's (out of my own chronological sequence of publications), the pattern of my experience, and Cameroon's, makes this the proper place to establish the *Abbia* paper's context and then to reproduce its text.

Because it fell dormant in 1982 and had little circulation outside Cameroon, I arrived there in 1989 ignorant of *Abbia*. But I found, early on, its entire run in the Bamenda cathedral's library (I never saw more than fragmentary *Abbia* collections elsewhere). Benefiting from this first of archbishop Paul Verdzekov's many kindnesses, I settled into regular "Bishop's House" visits and read completely through its 5,500 pages, beginning in 1989 and finishing in 1991, on the way to the 1996 text appearing here. Far exceeding the *Cameroon Cultural Review* descriptor in its title, *Abbia* proved to be a provocative and comprehensive source for every part of my culture-education-language-development research mantra. Education and language study in 1989 had required a circuitous, not always productive chase from one venue to another. By contrast, although meetings with many of the journal's principals were dispersed in time and space, taking me to Douala, Yaounde and Garoua, I read *Abbia* in tightly focused sequence. Its key people on the topic of culture turned out to be front line informants for education and language as well, and enriched my entire research enterprise.

William Eteki Mboumoua was a primary source. He had spent most of the 1960s as Ahidjo's minister of national education, youth and culture, was in that formal role also *Abbia*'s senior editor, and was the closest of its core creative group not only to domestic orbits of influence *Abbia* attracted and cultivated but also to an international talent base of contributors and of agencies like UNESCO that supported *Abbia* both intellectually and materially. Two others among Abbia's original creators, Eldridge Mohammadou and Marcien Towa, also remained available in 1989 for consultation across the range of my scholarship in person as well as print. Sadly, Bernard Nsokika Fonlon, their close Abbia colleague, as active in public life as Eteki Mboumoua, likewise a cabinet minister under Ahidjo, had died in 1986. One of his signature titles, *The Genuine Intellectual* (1978), told how the years around 1968 engaged him as an African on the ground in ways I could recognize as an incipient Africanist before I reached the continent, and he worked, taught and wrote voluminously on issues my research touched (as in Chapter 1 here). Lacking Fonlon's direct help as work on my *Abbia* manuscript continued until its 1996 appearance in print, but recognizing his centrality (like Tadadjeu's) to my entire domain of study, I was still able to access his work and career through his writings (six of them, spanning a quarter century, are now available in a 2012 Langaa edition, *The Task of Today and Other Seminal Essays*), family and other private sources in Bamenda, Fonlon Society members, and "legacy" publications about him in print by the mid-1990s.

Abbia was a singularly, richly diverse journal, for its content and its commentary, and was decisive for my appraisal of Cameroon's condition. Its quasi-"official" status, from *Abbia*'s ministerial funding to the connections of some early and later editorial board members to government, predisposed me to reservations about its autonomy. And Eteki Mboumoua, Ahidjo's original ministerial custodian at the journal, moderated his pioneer's enthusiasm with caution about *Abbia*'s purpose and prospects in its very first appearance: it would not be "a platform for immoderate invective, or…a forum for propounding partisan points of view." But its first decade was consistently, sometimes almost riotously provocative on public culture and policy issues, exemplified by Fonlon's early, Maoist invocation: "Let a hundred flowers blossom! Let a hundred schools of thought contend!" The first issue, for example, Eteki Mboumoua notwithstanding, dropped a stone not a pebble in the pool of language debate surveyed above, with an article by the career diplomat Jack Kisob advocating Pidgin as an official national language option despite its low prestige and scanty written heritage. It was after all, he argued, Cameroon's most widely spoken medium of communication, with potential like KiSwahili's in eastern Africa as a populist developmental force.

The language issue continued to animate *Abbia*, with a series of Fonlon's writings on language policy. He was an early advocate for and architect of Cameroon's authorized French-English bilingualism, not just for its specific historical relevance but as a hallmark and example of adaptive and creative modernity Cameroon could contribute to Africa's future capacities and prospects. He believed that the spread of bilingualism from "Africa's crossroads" in linguistic, cultural and geographical terms could give Cameroon a continental leadership niche and a unique destiny. But by *Abbia*'s fifth issue, 1964, in both French and English texts, citing Abraham Lincoln's "house divided" argument and phraseology, he attacked the policy's biased implementation. Ultimately, *Abbia* in 1978 published Fonlon's anathema against the French language domestically on bad faith and uneven preference grounds, concluding with his call for English, over time, to become "the first language of instruction in the University…and the first official language of Cameroon."

This was the fault line 1985's Open Letter and 1989's Etats-Généraux openly disclosed when I first arrived in Cameroon, and became a key diagnostic measure as my studies progressed. It demonstrated the impact of the 1972 referendum that turned Cameroon from a federal into a united republic, and of 1984's decree that removed cultural, educational, linguistic and constitutional, indeed all limitations, by adopting the single word "republic" to designate Cameroon. It was precisely, not randomly, in the referendum's year that Fonlon left ministerial office for the academy and made *Abbia* the lead forum for his cumulative critique of national governance and civic culture. Although the journal's critical force was otherwise diminished in its later issues, thunder rolled across Fonlon's final *Abbia* appearance in the "RES UNA PUBLICA" text of 1982, with its multiple anathemas that many anglophones I met in and after 1989 could quote verbatim. I read all of Fonlon's *Abbia* texts while Cameroon remained outwardly calm in 1989, and they alerted me to complexities in my field of study I would not have so clearly recognized without them. Fonlon was at least nominally equivocal about Ahidjo himself as the source of the country's deficits during his presidency, but his *Abbia* texts on the character and exercise of citizenship in a free polity, and the constraints Cameroon imposed, otherwise pulled no punches and influenced all my writings thereafter.

Fonlon was not alone on *Abbia's* critical front while it still flourished. Towa wrote in early issues about négritude as obscurantist, and of dependency on the French legacy, at a time when Léopold Senghor's influence shaped francophone African thinking and Ahidjo was courting him. Fonlon's close university counterpart as a man of letters and tribune, the francophone Thomas Melone, a veteran of student anti-colonial politics in France and post-colonial opposition in Cameroon, called for a reconstruction of higher education, away from civil service training and the professions of administration and law, into a more developmentally productive curriculum and pedagogy, in which the liberal arts and social sciences (broadly speaking, my own chief research interests at the time) would figure prominently as a check on "fonctionnarisme."

Such generic critiques and calls for systemic change were abroad in Cameroon in 1989, however limited the appetite for risk in the ranks of what a leading domestic scholar of politics, Pierre Flambeau Ngayap, had in 1983 described as "la classe dirigeante," 1,000 or so in number. But *Abbia's* ramparts were lower, and retrenchment on the critical front was apparent, as early as 1968. Its champion Eteki Mboumoua's role as minister of national education, youth and culture ended then, and the culture portfolio in Ahidjo's cabinet was shifted and became a ministerial adjunct of information. That ministry and

76

Abbia's masthead and interior pages over the next decade advanced people like Jacques Fame Ndongo, Hubert Mono Ndjana, Ebenezer Njoh Mouelle and Gervais Mendo Ze, often students of French semiotics and "new criticism," more narrowly Melone's functionaries, noticeably drawn more from Biya's own Beti ethnicity cluster than before.

Exceptions like Fonlon aside, *Abbia*'s vanguard critical and imaginative voices had lapsed before the journal ceased publication in 1982. Fame Ndongo's own 1988 book, *Le Prince et le scribe* (appearing a year after Biya's *Communal Liberalism*: was that a designed pairing?), applied Machiavelli to Cameroon, advocated guidance of the intelligentsia by state interests, can be read as a direct rebuttal of Fonlon, and foreshadowed a future in which Fame Ndango's informal influence and high offices accumulated. These two and their associates, Fonlon in eclipse, Fame Ndongo rising, were apt barometers for Cameroon by 1989, easily tapped in *Abbia* and echoed elsewhere, along the conceptual and experiential spectrum between open and closed societies, and about the tensions raised and the stakes involved.

Fonlon and Melone in particular had warned and worked against what had become more Fame Ndongo's Cameroon than theirs. Cameroon's official cultural apparatus thereafter inducted more and more functionaries. Fame Ndongo remains at the core of what the dissident scholar Ambroise Kom, in many ways Fonlon's and Melone's heir as well as the major advocate for Mongo Beti, Ahidjo's and then Biya's fiercest critic, would by 1991 brand as "organic intellectuals" engaged in a "mythification of power" on Biya's behalf. All this registered within the first ten days of my 1995 research trip, when I attended a Yaounde colloquium of cultural and political notables who were not uniformly dissidents and, as reported early in the *Abbia* text, heard them agree in general that the Cameroon state's "Gaullist" ways had now become "Vichist."

My *Abbia* writing, finally published in 1996, to which this preface now yields, covers all this and more; readers will be more amused than I and my editor were at the time by its one easily detected,

77

glaring French-to-English translation error. They will also recognize, more seriously, that those who shaped and directed Cameroon's public culture and its policy consequences in the wake of *Abbia*'s generation, the people holding sway by 1989-1991, and their heirs, though challenged in ways sketched here, remain dominant to this day, a quarter century later. I leave judgment about their role and influence on Cameroon's national development, and any sense of its vision, to each reader. My own bearings will be no secret.

Building the Republic through Letters: *Abbia: Cameroon Cultural Review*, 1963-82, and Its Legacy

Introduction

Cameroon's experience in the mid-1990s is among Africa's harshest. Its economy is diving from relative prosperity during the first quarter-century of independence since 1960-61 to what a 1995 World Bank study identified as a catastrophic performance since 1988. Its politics, one party in char- acter, 1966-90, then opened to multi-party reforms, are stalled in the wake of a disputed 1992 presidential election, with the incumbent regime of Paul Biya still in place and the main opposition Social Democratic Front party of John Fru Ndi keeping up pressure but unable to dislodge "le pouvoir." Its society is adrift, with no resolution of what this officially French-English bilingual nation knows generically as "la crise/the crisis."

For our purpose here, a study of *Abbia*, Cameroon's leading journal of culture, 1963-82, one episode among many registers the current sense of public affairs. There was a Yaounde colloquium on democratic transition and governance on 3 February 1995, staged and attended by the successors to the high echelon intelligentsia that was responsible for *Abbia* at its inception a generation before. From the audience, well versed in a critical vocabulary of the Cameroon state's "Gaullist" history, came a remark that it was now a "Vichist" state. Not a murmur of surprise or dissent followed; it was a characterization that circle took for granted, just a month past the 35th anniversary of independence for the former French trust territory, the first phase of nationhood before unification with the British region in the Federal Republic, 1961.

This striking note of dissatisfaction marks the failure to realize the promise and vision that audience's earlier peers vested so confidently in *Abbia*. Very early in Cameroon's national history, with the federation framed in principle during 1960-61 but by no means defined in practice, *Abbia: Cameroon Cultural Review* (the full title) appeared as the government's first major publication of this type. Conceived in 1962, first published in 1963, it flourished in the 1960s,

79

faltered by the latter 1970s, and finally lapsed in 1982. Its 20 years, 40 volumes, and some 5,500 pages, with a peak press run of 20,000, constitute one of Africa's most prolific and comprehensive efforts to document and shape a national culture through the medium of the scholarly periodical. Its guiding presence, Bernard Fonlon, told Stephen Arnold, near its end, that *"Abbia* is largely unknown even in Cameroon ..."* and it is probable that only a few thousand Cameroonians saw or read the journal consistently through its life (Arnold 56; Asanga interview). But the labors of both policy and love devoted to *Abbia* provide one of the continent's most striking examples of humane letters sustained in one journal over many years.

There is no doubt from the text of *Abbia* and my talks since 1989 with some of its surviving founders and early leaders (William Eteki Mboumoua, Marcien Towa, and Eldridge Mohammadou, but unfortunately not Fonlon, who died in 1986) that the formation of an intelligentsia committed to Cameroon state building priorities was President Ahmadu Ahidjo's strategy for the journal. Eteki Mboumoua as Minister of National Education, Youth and Culture until 1968 and Fonlon, posted in the presidency until 1964, then a Deputy Minister and Minister until 1971, were his channels as *Abbia's* effective founders. Their high offices immediately, inevitably, bring into play Jean-François Bayart's critique of African intellectuals operating within state structures:

> ... because they more readily lend their services to the state than to its challengers, African intellectuals (with few exceptions) have failed to provide civil society with the original conceptual instruments required for its advance. Even when they have had the courage to offer themselves to the leadership of the resistance, they have in no way been able to transcend the epistemic gulf between state and civil society. (qtd. in Chabal, 120)

The cogency of Bayart's judgment for *Abbia* and Cameroon must be an issue in this study, especially in light of the contest there since

1990 between state and civil society. For caution is needed when applying Bayart's remark about regimes and the intelligentsia. We demonstrate below that *Abbia* cannot be dismissed as Ahidjo's house organ until 1982, the year that the journal suspended publication and the president resigned. And one of the clear manifestations of the current political crisis, demonstrated at the Yaounde colloquium, is the bold challenge to and substantial erosion of the state's capacity to engage the loyalty of intellectuals, whom Biya, Ahidjo's successor since 1982, now finds increasingly fractious. Fonlon's principled independence, always stubborn, at times reckless, is attested by all who knew him in Ahidjo's time, and is reflected by the "Socrates in Cameroon" reputation he commanded, linking him to the classical world's icon of critical autonomy. Richard Bjornson left in his monumental 1991 study of Cameroon letters no doubt about Fonlon's firm, independent course for most of *Abbia's* history (Bjornson 174-77). This study will show the journal's considerable diversity and, for at least the first decade and a half, its persistent voice as alternative, even challenge, to Ahidjo's statecraft and the attendant public culture. Its last half-decade was less bold, and will yield some observations about how independence from and vigilance against state powers turned to proximity and compliance among Cameroon's intellectuals, thus aligning this study of *Abbia* with the critical perspective Bayart demands. Comparing *Abbia's* broad early scope and critical temper with its later limits serves well to demonstrate generic features of Cameroon's, and Africa's, problems in constructing and sustaining national cultures which close the gaps between its producers and consumers, its participants and spectators, those with high place and those with little or nothing to do with the workings of state policy in this as in other spheres.

Indeed, both autonomy and constraint figured in *Abbia's* mission articulated when its original creator, the Minister of National Education Eteki Mboumoua, wrote the preface to the first issue. On one hand, voicing the hopes of a generation of young African pioneers taking office at independence, he framed the broadest

81

possible manifesto, placing culture alongside the more obviously compelling factor in national development, technology:

> ... *Abbia* shall strive to preserve the factors native to Cameroon and African culture, to give them a life of their own in the new technical, modernist order ... the present period is, and should be, for us Africans, as meaningful as, or should I say, more intense than, the Renaissance in Europe. *Abbia* has arrived in time to enliven this Renaissance. *(Abbia* 1: 11-12; subsequent *Abbia* citations provide volume and page numbers only.)

At the same time, however, Eteki Mboumoua made clear what *Abbia* would *not* offer, in an excerpt enjoining caution just below the first masthead:

> Committed cultural action? Let's be clear about it. My role here shall be to see to it that *Abbia,* or any other publication, for that matter, with a similar mission, does not degenerate, on the pretext of freedom of cultural expression or on the pretext of commitment, into a platform for immoderate invective, or into a forum for propounding partisan points of view. There can be no culture worthy of the name without a progressive, serene, objective and consistent outlook. (1: 10)

Discourse, Cameroonians were here warned, should be contained within a "responsible" framework under state and ministry patronage.

Eteki Mboumoua praised Ahidjo for leaving *Abbia* to its own devices, as Fonlon praised Ahidjo, the minister, and the latter's early successors for respecting the editorial freedom he insisted on and was generally accorded. But any assessment of the journal over 20 years must balance the evidence of freedom and diversity in *Abbia's* pages against the range of excluded discourse and restricted agenda.

I. Abbia: Journal of Record and Voice for Renaissance

Abbia was a government venture that UNESCO, other non-Cameroonian sources, and non-governmental support sources within the country helped finance and produce (27-28: 16-17; Bjornson 174). It was determinedly Cameroon's face and voice. The title word, *Abbia,* designated, and the front cover of every issue displayed, seeds from southern Cameroon's forests, finely incised with people, flora, and fauna; the French had outlawed their use for gambling, making their appearance on *Abbia's* cover a symbolic liberation (38-40: 297). As visual backdrop to the seeds, and also on *Abbia's* back cover, was the script developed by the revered Sultan Njoya of Bamum (or Bamoun), also proclaiming indigenous values and defiance, since the French had 30 years earlier destroyed his printing press and exiled to Yaounde this innovator responsible for a clear challenge to French language monopoly (3: 30).

There was an *Abbia* editorial triumvirate into the early 1970s: the anglophone but fluently bilingual Fonlon of Nso ethnicity who was educated in Nigeria, England, Ireland, and France; the Beti francophone trained in France, Marcien Towa; Eldridge Mohammadou, a northern multilingual Anglo-Fulani schooled in Germany and France. They were diverse enough in geographic, ethnic, and linguistic origins to mirror Cameroon's diversity, and sufficiently cosmopolitan in their higher educations abroad to create a balanced and comprehensive national forum.

Abbia began prolifically, with four issues during 1963. They projected the optimism of that period's nation building agenda ("from many, one") and a wider Pan-African promise. Members of the editorial staff, not just the francophone majority but Fonlon as well, were acquainted or experienced with *Présence Africaine* and its networks, including frequent international colloquia, which challenged the residue of colonial African leadership during the 1950s. Successors to such colloquia were closely reported in *Abbia,* like the official continent-wide meetings since 1960 of newly empowered cabinet ministers with authority for policy touching education and culture, in Addis Ababa, Tananarive, and elsewhere. So were the large and numerous gatherings that UNESCO and other sponsors still convened for freelance writers and artists, teachers, and scholars. Thus, for example, Fonlon was able to attend and report on the 1962 Accra International Congress of Africanists, where the Nigerian historian Kenneth Dike presided and W. E. B. Du Bois made one of his last appearances, and the Kampala meeting of writers in 1963. This was pioneer work by determined Africans, meant in *Abbia* and similar publications to align national and continental cultures with the early 1960s political aspirations, indeed to indigenize and apply the experience of *Présence Africaine.*

Another dimension of this ambition and optimism was the continual documentation in *Abbia* of projects "made in Cameroon." Some were completely new and fully indigenous, although most supplanted or revised pre-independence ventures and relied on assistance from abroad. They were as large as the new Federal University and Ecole Normale Supérieure in Yaounde, as pointed in their nationalist trajectory as archives and research centers based on Cameroon materials and priorities and on new technology for their production and presentation, as locally pitched in their appeal to the new national order as the *West Cameroon Teachers Journal* replacing *Nigerian Teacher* for anglophones.

In the first years, therefore, and through most of its run, *Abbia's* pages projected the indigenous message of its covers, ranging the cultures of Cameroon in scholarly and popular form. Volumes 1-4, for instance, featured articles on Bassa legal customs, Nso and Bakweri religions, Bali costume; in most such cases practitioners and students from these populations were the authors. Perhaps the most impressive and prolific indigenous coverage in early *Abbia* was a series of literary and political texts and commentaries on the less-known peoples of northern Cameroon, the special concern of Mohammadou; they were provided him in Arabic, Fulfulde, and other northern languages, and he put them into French for *Abbia* (Arnold 53). Another distinctive feature of *Abbia's* mirror for Cameroon beside this diversity was the official bilingual policy

84

promoting both French and English. These early volumes, more than their successors, printed many special articles in both languages, as well as conventional articles in each of them. This was Fonlon's preoccupation, as very much the architect of a bilingualism meant both to bridge Cameroon's different peoples and to realize for Cameroon two of its possibilities, a unique competence in both languages and (thereby) a strategic "crossroads of Africa" destiny. *Abbia* first published his blueprint for the scheme in 1963, and a 1966 text specified Cameroon as Africa's "carrefour historique et culturel" (4: 56-94; 12-13: 63) 'historic and cultural crossroad.' A lesser known editor and contributor, Mbassi Manga, added to *Abbia's* and bilingualism's goal of "one personality writing indifferently in French and English" the hope that the journal could also privilege other languages, for those in Cameroon not yet within the immediate reach of the two official languages (2: 16). *Abbia,* in fact, consistently advanced their appearance, using three or four indigenous languages in some volumes, five of them in 1965's double Volume 9-10. It also included in Volume 1 a paper advocating Pidgin as a language worth support, defending it against the scorn of most intellectuals by pointing out its wide popular use and its future as a national language with distinctive political and creative potential, like KiSwahili's (1: 25-30).

Fonlon's use of Mao--"Let a hundred' flowers blossom! Let a hundred schools of thought contend!"--and Mbassi Manga's own phrase--"Our cultural laboratory is ready for new inventions"--aptly projected Cameroon's and *Abbia's* early faith (2: 12, 17). The journal was the nation's showcase, rich in talent, broad in outlook, experimental, celebratory. Its verve and virtuosity were demonstrated in the 1963 contributions by the physical chemist Michel Doo Kingue on jazz, from its origins to the latest works of John Coltrane, while Doo Kingue was in transit from his pioneer Cameroon theater project in Paris to a UNESCO career directing its technical services by the time he retired in 1992 (2: 122-134; 3: 133-140). If there was one gap, less obvious at the time than now, it was the virtually total lack of women's contributions at all levels. Commentary from Lilyan

Kesteloot, the Belgian scholar teaching at Yaounde, poems from students at a Garoua lycée, and a moving eulogy on the early death of a staff member and potentially larger voice, Ruth Belinga, provide a merely skeletal textual base.

Ahidjo had good reason, on the evidence of the early output profiled here, and in succeeding volumes for some time, to give *Abbia* its head. Interestingly, the young Paul Biya's name was on the editorial board while he was Eteki Mboumoua's Director of Cabinet, volumes 1-4, an apprenticeship in the linkage of letters to statecraft worth noting.

II. Letters and Statecraft: A Critique Emerges

Apart from standard complaints about the colonial grip on culture, not quickly enough released, only one critical voice, that of Marcien Towa, surfaced that first year, but Towa's concern was noticeable and constituted the first evidence of combativeness as *Abbia* settled in. In an article on colonial education's legacy, which introduced his own distinctively critical voice and paved the way for others, he called Yaounde's European and American cultural centers subtle and cunning Trojan horses (3: 33-34). A more fundamental critique soon followed. By early 1964, in the lead article format which gave readers the sense of the editorial board's or his own special word, Fonlon issued the first of the jeremiads which made his reputation as Cameroon's conscience. "Will We Make or Mar?/Construire ou détruire?" introduced volume 5 in both languages by warning that Cameroon's vision was in jeopardy. Using as preface a passage from Lincoln's "house divided" text, he documented the failure to apply bilingualism in the even-handed way necessary for successful implementation of the policy and integration of the nation's indigenous, French and British cultures, as distinct from French assimilation (5: 9, 12-14). Here, *Abbia's* architect, Fonlon, condemned his client, Ahidjo. Criticizing the assimilationist creed, contrasting it pointedly with the integrationist need, he warned that, against the grain of agreements about federal guarantees which Fonlon himself helped negotiate at Cameroon's inception, "we will all be French in two generations or three," if policy did not change (5: 12).

Thus, readers moving from Volume 4 to 5 found Fonlon defending the foundations of his bilingual policy in a way unmistakably directed at those he feared would never carry it into practice, Ahidjo and the state apparatus. Citing "French cultural hegemony" and the French antipathy to all things African, he singled out for an exemplary warning Cameroon's most prominent new institution, Yaounde's Federal University:

·... you can take it for granted that it will be a French university, pure and simple, if the Cameroon authorities do not take this institution well in hand ...

and compared it unfavorably to Nigeria's University of Ibadan. There, he argued, British origins provided both genuine African leadership and a foreign presence constructive in its cosmopolitanism, not (like Yaounde) harboring a narrow, destructive European influence (5: 25-26).

These lines of criticism initiated and' sustained by both Towa and Fonlon intensified throughout the 1960s. Fonlon himself returned often to these themes, first in volume 11 (1965) with "Idea of Culture," a discussion of Africa informed by a survey of classical models of how to inculcate virtue and avoid vice. Turning to contemporary Africa, he found

> ... a spectacle disheartening and discouraging. At this stage, when the dawn of African independence is just breaking, evils which would normally come with decline and exhaustion have already overtaken us and are eating their way deep into the vitals of the body politic--corruption, embezzlement, grasping individualism, cynical indifference to the general welfare. (11: 27)

He then turned to higher education's mission:

> ... we need men of high learning and specialized skill ... But ... seeing the extreme misery of the African masses, how can those dedicated to the cause of redeeming these masses fulfil their mission duly, if they shrink back from descending into hell? The situation calls for ... austere asceticism in the lives of the African elite and leadership. (11: 27)

Fonlon's reference here to Cameroon and its conduct of politics and education, so compelled by his sense of calling on both fronts (nurtured by long Catholic seminary apprenticeship) was implicit. Quite explicit was his resort to writings against imposed forms of education by Ireland's Padraic Pearse and India's Mohandas Gandhi, nationalist rebels who made those descents from elite to mass surroundings Fonlon called for and were respectively executed and jailed for their efforts. Their resistance served Fonlon as models for Africa's leaders (11: 20-22).

A year later *Abbia* printed a bluntly explicit critique of Cameroon's university, bridging and extending Towa and Fonlon, which left no doubt about its failure thus far to serve society. Thomas Melone was the first Cameroonian appointed to the Federal University's faculty, as head of a new Department of Comparative African Literature, which made his "Université, Multiversité et développement économique (Réflexions sur l'Université Federale du Cameroun)" especially interesting. He cited "les dangers du fonctionnarisme" (14-15: 115) and argued that Yaounde's early tendencies threatened to direct limited resources to the irreversibly unproductive use of donors' and taxpayers' investments:

> Naturellement tant que nos universités africaines continueront à se considérer comme des machines à fonctionnaires, leurs structures ne varieront pas, parce que la saturation du secteur administratif et la modicité des ressources publiques entraîneront un ralentissement automatique mais comprehensible de la formation des cadres et une paupérisation objective de la masse des contribuables. (14-15: 116)

> Naturally, so long as our African universities continue to regard themselves as machines producing civil servants, their structures will not change, because the saturation of the administrative sector and the low level of public resources will entail an automatic but understandable slowing down of the training of cadres and a real pauperization of the taxpayers.

He proposed, before it was too late, based on practices known from his research and travel as a ranking scholar at Yaounde, open access to the university which a targeted tax revenue like Brazil's could provide, flexible funding including private sector sources, and use like the University of Nigeria (Nsukka)'s of the American land grant model to promote continuing and applied education. These were moves Melone thought could divert Yaounde from a major consequence of "[c]ette philosophie du fonctionnarisme ... la fiction que l'Etat pouvait tout faire à la fois" (14-15: 116-121) 'this civil service philosophy ... the fiction that the State could do everything at once.' Otherwise, conditions at the present time (1966) would be fixed forever: a university student body so skewed toward "fonctionnarisme" rather than productivity that the faculty of law (with economics also as its purview) enrolled 581 students against science's 85; the virtually total neglect of indigenous research as a base for faculty support, publication and promotion (14-15: 119,125; see 19: 21 for Fonlon's counter-example of his Nso colleague Daniel Lantum's research on medicinal traditions of great potential).

Melone's critique remains valid in the mid-1990s on both these counts. Meanwhile, as *Abbia* recorded and interpreted the 1960s, its skeptical scrutiny of both institutional and intellectual bearings in Cameroon intensified. A body of criticism increasingly framed *Abbia's* "journal of record" repertoire for national culture.

Thus, there appeared in Volume 19 (1968), perhaps the journal's single most contentious issue, a translation of Wole Soyinka's *The Lion and the Jewel* and an introductory essay on Soyinka by the French scholar Philippe Laburthe-Tolra. He located in Soyinka the free spirit whom prison could not silence, and the critic on one hand of Léopold Senghor as Négritude advocate, on the other of Kwame Nkrumah as autocrat, using the play which anticipated his fall, *Kongi's Harvest*. This was the crux of the argument:

[I]l risque de s'aliéner l'instituteur, le roi, Ie fonctionnaire, le président, le prêtre, le général, mais en definitive, seulement ceux d'entre eux qui sont sots, et la part intelligente de la société l'

90

applaudira .... Encore paralysée ... l' Afrique d'aujourd'hui manque d'auteurs comiques qui traduisent ... ce bon sens critique populaire, cette acuité de l' observation et cette gaieté caricaturale .... L' Afrique a besoin de ce rire qui lui est à la fois si naturel et si traditionnel. (19: 65)

> [H]e risks alienating the teacher, the king, the civil servant, the president, the priest, the general, but finally only those among them who are fools, whereas the intelligent part of society will applaud him ...Still paralyzed ... Africa today lacks comic writers who express ... this critical popular good sense, this sharpness of observation, and this caricatural mirth .... Africa needs this laughter which is at once so natural and so traditional to it.

Cameroon too, he specified, needed the ridicule of a Moliere, and he hinted at Voltaire's "Ecrasez l'infâme!" as the more sovereign remedy, the cultural and political antidote Soyinka prescribed.

This was provocative, unmistakably a commentary on the French scholar's experience of Yaounde and Cameroon. It served to introduce Towa's several volleys of criticism during 1968-69, which followed Ahidjo's tightened censorship law and creation of a single party politics under Cameroon National Union auspices. *Abbia's* editorial meetings may have been volatile in this period as Towa challenged Ahidjo, for Fonlon was successively Cameroon's Deputy Foreign Minister, Minister of Transport, Posts and Telecommunications, and Minister of Public Health and Social Welfare.

Very much a controversialist, whose merits took him quickly up the ranks of scholarship and academic administration in the 1960s, Towa's dissent intensified when *Abbia* in 1968 reproduced his 1967 lecture at the Ecole Normale Supérieure, His "Civilisation industrielle et négritude" attacked Senghor for a "pathétique antinomie . . . statique, raciste" of thought, for isolating technical and cultural capacities, and for denying the possibility and efficacy of their conjunction (19: 32). The dichotomy, Towa argued, was deterministic

91

on biological grounds, falsified Africa, and could be historically refuted by attention to interactions past and present which showed dynamics like Egypt's heritage in classical Greece and Europe's in modem Japan, transmitting "technique" and leaving indigenous cultures viable (19: 45).

Whereas Ahidjo promoted Cameroonian support for Senghor and Négritude, Towa challenged this posture and rubbed salt by aligning himself with the critiques of Senghor and Sartre by anti-Ahidjo forces like the exiled Cameroonian novelist Mongo Beti and the dissident Fédération des Etudiants d' Afrique Noire in Paris: Beti was *persona non grata* at home, and this was in fact the only reference to him I have found in *Abbia* (Bjornson 170-205, for background; 19: 33). For Towa, the issue was not African technical incapacity but the specific character of colonial transactions, including the still pervasive foreign "technical advisors" who denied or frustrated Africa's proven capacity to adapt, Towa's term for what Fonlon called "integration" (19: 41). Building on less bluntly polemical writing we have sampled in *Abbia* from Fonlon and Melone, Towa augmented the details of Cameroon's continued reliance and dependence on the French in particular" for "modern" initiatives, and made Ahidjo's approach look neocolonial and, moreover, imitative of Senghor's, rather than liberating.

Next in Towa's *Abbia* arsenal was "Le Consciencisme: émergence de l' Afrique moderne à la conscience philosophique" in Volume 20. It was first written in France in 1964, rebutting an essay in *Le Monde* that referred to reservations about Ghana's president and his 1963 text, *Consciencism,* among young intellectuals. Published unaltered in *Abbia* in 1968, the essay therefore read differently than Laburthe-Tolra's use of Soyinka against Nkrumah in the previous issue. Towa framed Nkrumah as a foil against Senghor, citing enthusiastic support for his thought and policy, as far removed from Senghor's as could be. The argument was intricate, founded on pre-Socratic materialism, used in *Consciencism* as a base for what modem philosophy ought to be, absent the veils of idealism and religion, and which Towa used as a model for Africa's escape from "Bantu philosophy" and the obscurantist shackles it forged (20: 5-19). This made Nkrumah, not Senghor, the exemplar for a philosophy which would stress the active rather than inert character of both thought and social forces in Africa, and would constitute challenges to the party and state structures emerging there in the 1960s (20: 30).

This was certainly a challenging *Abbia* "intervention" from the Cameroonian philosopher, by now influential across the curriculum at Yaounde's Ecole Normale Supérieure. Having surveyed philosophy as it touched statecraft in a way critical of current African leadership, Towa devoted the article's last pages to a familiar litany of neocolonial abuse, adding for good measure the issue of French nuclear tests in Africa and the opposition to them which Nkrumah organized, against the silence of French-backed heads of state.

We may be confident that Towa's denials of Senghor and his eminence were also meant to diminish Ahidjo; they appeared as greater and lesser *arrivistes* in these texts. He did not relent. Following an Ecole Normale Supérieure colloquium on Aimé Césaire in 1968, two more *Abbia* articles in 1969 advanced Towa's polemic by denying Senghor's oft-cited bond with Césaire. Volume 21's "Aimé Césaire: prophète de la révolution des peuples noirs" in fact linked Césaire not to Senghor but to his comrade from Martinique Frantz Fanon, a striking frame of comparison to Ahidjo's Cameroon, where *maquisard* resistance against the regime and its French support base still survived. Towa discovered in Cesaire "la rélation passionnée du victorieux combat spirituel livre par un 'damné de la terre' pour démolir la ténéreuse prison idélogique où il était tenu captif" (21: 50) 'the impassioned account of the successful spiritual combat delivered by a "wretched of the earth" in order to demolish the gloomy ideological prison where he was held captive.' He then used Césaire's 1956 text *Culture et colonisation* to argue the latter's independence of a number of derivative influences which he claimed Senghor embraced:

> ... il réfuse de biologiser le culturel ... de revendiquer une supériorité innée du Nègre ...

93

... he refuses to biologize the realm of culture ... as a way to claim an innate superiority for the Black ...

and then freed Césaire as the black world's voice from Marx as well as Senghor:

Un prolétaire peut devenir bourgeois, mais un Nègre ne saurait franchir totalement la ligne de separation des races. (21: 50-53)

A proletarian can become bourgeois, but a Black will not be able totally to cross the line separating the races.

This capacity to transcend both Négritude and Marxism was the theme of Towa's second 1969 contribution on Cesaire in Volume 23. "Les Pur-sang: Négritude Césairienne et Surréalisme" used a poem Cesaire first published in *Tropiques* (1942), later the cornerstone for *Armes Miraculeuses* (1946), to argue that Césaire experienced an epiphany that in 1941 liberated him from all obscurantist limits of black perception. The occupation of Martinique that year by Vichy forces made a relatively distant and relaxed post of empire confront "le triomphe du nazisme et du fascisme" that not just the familiar French planter elites but also the fleet's common sailors imposed (21: 72). The resistance Césaire undertook led him, Towa argued, to a new language and consciousness, "une zone incandescent de révolte et de sécurité" (21: 72). Poetically and politically challenged in this encounter by both race and class foes, Césaire in Towa's view emerged as a uniquely liberated and universal writer and actor, beyond a black agenda and con- sciousness (21: 78). Ending the essay with a flourish which bridged Césaire in 1941 to contemporary Africa, these were Towa's last words:

Son dessein sera pleinement accompli le jour ou des voix noires ... exprimeront le coeur et l'esprit de nos peuples en une langue africaine. (21: 82)

His purpose will be fully achieved the day when black voices ... will express the heart and spirit of our peoples in an African language.

Towa's essays on Nkrumah and Césaire, targeting Senghor and Ahidjo, were in fact highly ambiguous. One was written about Nkrumah and a text, *Consciencism,* for which his authorial claim is disputed, and it is unclear whether or not Towa knew or chose to acknowledge that Ghana's Convention Peoples' Party and Nkrumah himself were notorious for the autocracy Towa obviously challenged in Cameroon when writing this essay in 1964, then reproducing it in 1968. It was published unchanged well after Nkrumah's 1966 fall from power, without any clear reading of Towa's attitude to current events in Ghana. It is possible in the second essay, as with his appropriation of Nkrumah against Senghor, to question Towa's use of Césaire against Senegal's president. Senghor also knew a full measure of wartime internment, and Césaire was by the time Towa wrote from Cameroon a fixture in France's National Assembly.

These are points to consider in another context, as Towa's Cameroonian critics do. We have identified with Towa, joined by others, a somewhat veiled but still remarkably trenchant line of criticism against Ahidjo's state leadership, intensified in the late 1960s, in Cameroon's leading subsidized journal of culture and opinion. Towa's consistent run of *Abbia* writings ended in 1969, as he began to encounter the consequences of his criticisms, and took time in France to complete his Doctorat d'Etat. There was one more attack on Senghor in his last *Abbia* essay, 1978: "Le senghorisme, c' est l' autoportrait du colonisé ... il nous fixe dans notre condition présente" (31-33: 44-45).

It was Fonlon, earlier less polemical in tone and categorical in judgment than Towa, who kept *Abbia* critically aligned to culture and politics in the 1970s. It is worth noting the timing of the works now to be cited; they began to appear in 1972 following his removal from cabinet posts to the university and the suddenly organized referendum which created the United Republic and ended federal powers in the anglophone West Cameroon state he had nurtured for a decade.

"To Every African Freshman" was a continuing series; the third installment, in volume 26, nominally on the nature of universities, turned into a close scrutiny of intellectuals in service to the state, historically and in contemporary Africa. He deplored, like Melone, the demonstrable careerism and concern for preferment which (in his own earlier language) already marred African universities, and admonished those complacent enough to be "a mindless cog in the wheel of any Establishment" and to heed "the insidious seductions of power" (26: 15). The instrumentalism of French African approaches to "la formation des cadres" drew his particular scorn (26: 23). Yet, he argued, drawing on a wide range of exemplars, from Socrates to Gandhi and the Nigerian Nnamdi Azikiwe, the intellectual must take the risk of working with those in power:

> ... [T]he genuine thinker-scholar ... must become, inevitably, the Keeper of the Public Conscience ... of Society ... in emerging Africa . . . should the intellectual take part in politics? My answer is unhesitating and unequivocal: Yes. (26: 28-29)

Citing the flattery and self-delusion he had witnessed among his writer peers at gatherings in Africa since independence, and their taste for proximity to politics' "back-room boys" in Cameroon, Fonlon concluded that "an intellectual ... should never forget that his central mission in politics is to be the Conscience and not merely the Agent of society ... merely and simply, the apologist of the status quo" (26: 30-33).

This text preferring gadflies to drones was not in itself remarkable; it was conventional enough in rhetoric and style, and avoided much reference to Cameroon. But when linked with his next major *Abbia* article in 1975, it reveals Fonlon's emerging critique of the state he had served so closely for a decade. "Le devoir d'aujourd'hui" in volume 29-30 opened by deploring modern government everywhere for making lies and propaganda so basic to the state's conduct, and the retention of power so much the politician's creed. At least in Europe, he added, there were publications like *Le Canard Enchaîné,* but Africa could not yet summon the ridicule and satire that challenged and exposed the abuse (29-30: 21-26).

From this opening commentary he turned to a long analysis of governance which set him clearly against the practice obtaining in Cameroon in recent years. There should be a separation rather than concentration of powers, and the British parliamentary style which had shaped West Cameroon until its destruction in the hastily called referendum of 1972 was his model. Moreover, features now advanced in Cameroon, "le parti unique" and "le régime présidentiel ... [tendent à] accorder à nos gouvernements une plus grande autorité" (29-30: 39-40). Advocating legislative initiatives and judicial checks against the executive, this was Fonlon's central conviction:

> Cette doctrine selon laquelle . . . l'Etat être doit place sur un pied d'égalité avec le simple citoyen ... est ... la plus sure sauvegarde de la démocratie. (29-30: 42-43)

> This doctrine according to which ... the State ought to be placed on equal footing with the ordinary citizen ... is ... the surest safeguard of democracy.

It was by no means a weak state he advocated, for the latter part of the text made Fonlon's case (in repeated italics and capital letters) for the WELFARE STATE and SOCIALISME DEMOCRATIQUE, in order to repatriate colonial economies, serve African populations' basic needs, and level inequalities already in place. But it was an accountable state he saw slipping away and wanted to preserve in Cameroon. Harold Laski was the essay's single most prominent source, Norway was its key example of balanced social democracy, the former West Cameroon state's Cameroon Development Corporation was its model public enterprise (29-30: 59-67).

97

This persistent web of texts from Fonlon and Towa, one the chief editor of *Abbia* for its two decades, the other his ranking deputy, both of them along with Eldridge Mohammadou the journal's most prolific contributors, demonstrates the journal's independence, and the state's tolerance. And the president's tolerance too, noted by Fonlon when Ahidjo received an honorary law degree from the national university in 1978:

> *Abbia* has waxed and waned, and waxed truculent…thanks to his Statecraft … his Statesmanship … his legendary patience, his tolerance, his generosity, yea, thanks to his active encouragement! … personally, and through his Ministers … he has often come to our aid … without the slightest thought of tampering with our freedom … from the first day to this. (31-33: 5-6).

Additionally, Fonlon used this occasion to state that "nobody with an honest mind will deny that the positive side of President Ahidjo [sic] twenty years' record is impressive, unquestionably."

But that qualifier "positive" was ambiguous, allowing for a negative side to the record, and Fonlon in 1978's *Abbia* was again the critic of much of Cameroon's culture in Ahidjo's time. There was a reference to himself, interesting in light of Eteki Mboumoua's original preface to the journal, as "a humanist among technologists" in government until his departure in 1971. Then came a long comparison, sketched (as noted above) in an earlier issue, now more fully detailed, favoring the University of Ibadan with its smaller constituent colleges, generalist course of studies, political independence, and versatile graduates like Achebe, to the French model "cité universitaire" which shaped the university at Yaounde (31-33: 7, 15, 36-46, 53, including references to the diversity and success of the Nigerian authors Aluko and Ekwensi, an engineer and pharmacist respectively).

He then brought into this 1978 issue of *Abbia,* from speeches previously delivered but unpublished, an alteration of the bilingual policy with French-English parity he had created which was far more startling and sweeping than some previous amendments he had suggested. Arguing that English now surpassed French as a global language, Fonlon registered his "firm conviction ... that English ... should increasingly become the first language of instruction in the University; indeed, that it should be elected as the first official language of Cameroon" (31-33: 46-52 for the full argument, 48 for the quoted passage). For good measure, Fonlon included a passage which seems gratuitous unless his five years at the university following his removal from government provoked it:

> I believe that, in the academy, rule should belong to Professors, and that, therein, princes should do homage. I believe that for Professors to merit this homage, for them to ward off the prince's interference in academics, their learning should be solid, their disinterestedness, towards non-intellectual power, beyond all shade of doubt ... (31-33: 52)

Fonlon's *Abbia* valedictory, in what turned out to be its last issue, commemorating the 10th anniversary of the United Republic, 1982, the year of Ahidjo's retirement as well, was as critical on a wide front in its early pages as any of Towa's earlier, more rhetorically charged yet more oblique thrusts at cultural politics in Cameroon. This text, "Res Una Republica," examined the public record since independence, and clearly distinguished and judged two methods and philosophies of statecraft by comparing "the Oneness of a State ... that is not simple, not monolith [but] composite ... a united whole" (38-40: 14). Fonlon used a blunt reference to the clash between Charles I's divine right kingship and Cromwell's Commonwealth, an injunction favoring "Humble Service not Haughty Power," and a plea for good government, such that "by surrounding monarch or president with solid institutions, with brain and integrity, by making King or President subject to the law, the abuse of power will be reduced to the minimum" (38-40: 14-21). This was unmistakable commentary on executive rule in Cameroon since the 1972 referendum. The next eight pages constituted Fonlon's reflections on

Ahidjo, full of praise for early nation-building efforts but also recognizing "a catalogue of abuses of power by some of his closest henchmen" (38-40: 22-29). "The President knows nothing of this" was his consistent line. But the impression of good intentions marred by flawed conduct was pervasive, and later parts of the text included a series of "anathema" pronouncements against those who misrule. They are, nearly two decades later, remembered, even quoted, by Cameroonians who consider Fonlon's arguments for limits on power prophetic and use his writings and reputation to justify resistance to Biya's presidency, which succeeded Ahidjo's the year *Abbia* last appeared.

III. "...A progressive, serene, objective and consistent outlook"

We now return to the statement quoted earlier, warning against invective and partisanship, which Eteki Mboumoua used to qualify the freedom granted *Abbia* from its inception, ending with the passage immediately above which favored moderation and a certain distance from any cultural wars. On evidence presented thus far, the journal in fact *was* engaged and developed critically, sometimes by inference, sometimes openly--certainly, for most of its two decades, beyond the shadow cast by Eteki Mboumoua's yellow light.

But there were also contributions which mirrored official viewpoints, and the most salient note prior to coverage *of Abbia* writings that fell within Cameroon's official political comfort zone is the virtually total absence in its pages of those writers whom Bjornson *inter alia* placed on the oppositionist wing. Bjornson built a conscious polarity in Cameroon writers' bearings between Ahidjo and the resistance leader killed before independence, Ruben urn Nyobe, as competing models for their loyalty. Many who, joining their leader Mongo Beti, "remembered Ruben" as a hero faced difficulty at home or were in expatriate and exile ranks abroad under Ahidjo, and so were not part of the national culture framed by *Abbia*.

The exceptions were sufficiently rare and fleeting to prove the rule. We noted earlier Beti's one and only appearance from his exile, in a particularly defiant Towa essay, despite his clearly first rank status as a Cameroonian writer in both imaginative and critical modes. There was also the case of Philippe-Louis Ombedé, better known as Rene Philombe, an *Abbia* editor during the 1960s, perhaps because he was president of the Association of Cameroonian Poets and Writers, which helped produce the journal. Though a far more prolific and respected writer than many *Abbia* published, his voice appeared there only in a 1978 interview with Bjornson, never in his own creative work (31-33: 213, 223). Another isolated glimpse of the disaffected (in Bjornson's terms) was a 1982 review of the work of the dramatist Alexandre Kuma Ndumbe III (38-40: 332-45). Otherwise, *Abbia* was no place for the truly recalcitrant critic, whether domestic, expatriate, or exile, occasional fiery poems in later issues like Babila Mutia's 1982 "Gong of Nemesis" notwithstanding (38-40: 129-30).

A scan of what *was* printed will indicate how *Abbia* provided the state, party, and presidency some comfort, increasingly so in its last issues as Ahidjo's application of statecraft isolated and marginalized Fonlon and victimized Towa, the two figures most responsible for the journal's critical pitch and maturity. As early as the same 1964 volume containing Fonlon's "Make or Mar" challenge, a recent returnee from the USA and Rutgers University published "Information: A Government Concern." Makoko-Makeba argued here that the purpose of government information services and opinion channels, which its state funds certainly made of *Abbia*, was "to build a reservoir of goodwill and support for the government" and that "Government must create in its citizens that diffuse sense of attachment which political philosophers call loyalty." He explicitly looked forward to a "ministry of information, as mouthpiece of government" (5: 109-10).

Such channeling was *not* consonant with *Abbia's* texts or editorial direction at the time, or later, but the article raised the question of *Abbia's* milieu, its congeniality to dissent, and the journal's future. Consider the evolution of ministerial structures in its area of coverage. At birth, it rested on the initiative and writ of Eteki Mboumoua, with the title Minister of National Education, Youth and Culture. The ministry remained so configured until 1968, and in Fonlon, Towa, Mohammadou, and the rest of its early principals, *Abbia* relied on collectively broad learning and experience abroad, including nationalist student movements with radical leanings in culture and politics, and domestically plural roots. Education and culture, when joined this way in ministerial policy focus and responsibility, in such hands, kept *Abbia* free to experiment and criticize. Makoko-Makeba's "information" in those years was bracketed with tourism in a small ministry whose function was culturally and politically innocuous. But from 1968 there was a Ministry of Information and Culture (note the sequence), and it became the bailiwick of appointees loyal--no, vigilant--about state and party in Makoko-Makeba's sense. For the next quarter-century, insofar as the two functions could be separated, Information dominated Culture in that ministry's work, and it was among Cameroon's foremost agencies of regime authority, quite at odds with *Abbia's* pioneers' goals. When opposition emerged in 1990, one concession to critics was an independent Ministry of Culture created in 1991 in the wake of a widely publicized national forum on culture. But rather than seeking and sponsoring new creative energies and perhaps relaxing some tensions in cultural politics, it languished, with obscure leadership and a miniscule budget, kept in shadows by the enhanced Ministry of Communications, which subsumed Information, directed state media, and was totally politicized to regime specifications. This was part of the backdrop to the "Vichist" state remark in 1995.

So was "Presidentialism," whether Gaullist or Vichist, the key for so long to Cameroon's political matrix, and always a factor shaping *Abbia's* sensitive role, and many responses to it. The journal was one of Ahidjo's showcases, a measure of his credentials. He lacked much formal education or pretensions to formal culture, but *Abbia* was a vehicle where his patronage could be demonstrated and a sense of his own as well as Cameroon's force in Africa could be projected. Fonlon was known as his channel to anglophones in particular and Cameroonians at large, quite literally as the eloquent source of speeches while at the presidency and in cabinet posts; *Abbia* was their joint venture for domestic and continental proof that Cameroon had "arrived." In 1967, for example, *Abbia* closely recorded both the first of Senghor's three visits to Cameroon between 1966 and 1973 and what it orchestrated, Cameroon's contributions to the First World Festival of Negro Arts in Dakar (12-13: 13-71). "Le Cameroun: Microcosme de la Négritude" was the dominant theme, and it served to align Ahidjo to Senghor in the most luminous possible way for Ahidjo.

Such ventures were important, staking claims for Ahidjo's reputation and historical legacy at the very time when Cameroon's

103

reality included ferocious warfare which France directed against pockets of maquisard resistance to his rule, and the increasingly monolithic state and single party Cameroon National Union. Those factors threatened to produce a less benign image. This complex political dynamic may account for *Abbia's* freedoms from control. As it turned most critical in 1968, it indirectly but distinctly served the president and his entire state apparatus, by projecting a sense of tolerance for dissent which cost the regime nothing. It was surely no coincidence that, as demonstrated above, the most fundamentally critical stream of material *Abbia* ever published began to appear in the next issues, with Towa and Fonlon the catalysts. They were not interfered with at the time.

But their leadership weakened through the 1970s, by attrition and pressure. Fonlon was there to the end. But Towa's travels from and travails within Cameroon, including dismissal from the university, reduced his role. He was substantially replaced on the journal and at the university by a scholar, Ebenezer Njoh-Mouelle, whose later political career we will trace below, and who was the source of the following commentary on Cameroon's experience, printed in *Abbia*, 1971:

Il appartient principalement à tout Etat de produire les remèdes nécessaires aux maux dont souffre la société. (25: 24)

It is principally up to every State to produce the necessary remedies to the evils from which society suffers.

Such *étatisme* was not Fonlon's now more lonely voice at *Abbia*, nor Towa's. Nor was it Melone's, whom we have seen mocking "la fiction que l'Etat pouvait tout faire à la fois" in 1966; he too was driven from the university, spent several years in French exile, then returned to his village to build a fishing enterprise, but disappeared from Cameroon's politics and culture until the late 1980s. Additionally, Eldridge Mohammadou decided by the mid-1970s that Yaounde was no place for productive work, moved his base of

104

research to Garoua, and contributed scholarship to *Abbia* from afar but not editorial guidance on the spot. His exemplary work site was among those abolished by a 1991 presidential decree citing budget reasons but commonly viewed as a way to disperse dissident intellectuals, and it was immediately vandalized; he left Cameroon and made Maiduguri in neighboring Nigeria the home of his still formidable scholarship.

Fonlon's thunder aside, *Abbia's* force waned. What it might have been beyond the 1970s--home of a cosmopolitan group of mature, potentially elder intellectual statesmen, steeped in nationalist movements abroad in the 1950s, seasoned by the experimental and optimistic enterprise of the 1960s at home, shielded thereafter by Ahidjo's needs and Fonlon's reputation--*Abbia* did not become. Nor, unlike what *Présence Africaine* did for *Abbia,* was the latter able to serve as an effective apprenticeship base for a fresh generation.

We have seen many factors in Cameroon's institutional fabric, especially after 1970, working to diminish *Abbia's* frequency and trenchancy: the press law and the creation of the one party state by 1967; the referendum for the unitary state in 1972; the ministerial realignments. Perhaps most salient, especially after Biya succeeded Ahidjo in 1982, was the extension of what Melone called "fonction-narisme" into a full blown employment and patronage system linking the university, the government media, and the ministries, party, and presidency. This factor was best illustrated in the careers of Ebenezer Njoh-Mouelle, Jacques Fame Ndongo, and Gervais Mendo Ze from 1980. All earned high academic degrees in France, returned to take up key academic posts at the University of Yaounde by the age of 30, and became published writers and current event essayists; Fame Ndongo's work was the most scholarly. Their profile superficially resembled that for the "re-entry class" c. 1960, but the experience and mentality were narrower, yielding different alignments and results.

We have emphasized Njoh-Mouelle's 1971 "Il appartient principalement à tout état ..." text; he published in *Abbia* from the late 1960s, and served as an editor for a decade from 1968. The 1971

105

passage was prophetic, for he became a mainstay in the circle of scholars who joined Biya directly in governance after 1982, eventually for three years as the Secretary-General of Biya's successor single party to Ahidjo's, the Cameroon People's Democratic Movement. His defeat in the legislative election of 1992 removed him from frontline politics, but he soon returned to an advisory post in the presidency.

Fame Ndongo's is the most instructive career, although he is the only one of these three never publicly associated with *Abbia*. A specialist in communications generally, in semiotics and journalism more specifically, his first domestic academic base was as Director of the university's "grande école" for mass communications, a role he maintained into the 1990s. He has also been at different times "Chargé de Mission" at the presidency and chief editor of the government daily *Cameroon Tribune* newspaper, effectively a monopoly until political pressure in 1990 forced a repeal of the 1966 press law and opened journalism to scores of competitors, many fiercely independent but subject to various forms of prior censorship and post-publication seizures. His major text, *Le prince et le scribe (1988)* argued to the following neo-Machiavellian conclusion for Africa:

> Un consensus est nécessaire: que le scribe accepte la nécessité de L'Etat et que le Prince favorise le débat d'idées, source de progrès et rempart contre la sclérose de l'Etat .... C'est la condition *sine qua non* d'un progrès authentique et durable. Ceci ne signifie pas que la fonction du scribe soit, par essence, de s'opposer ou de critiquer. (320)

> A consensus is necessary: let the scribe accept the need for the State and let the Prince encourage the debate of ideas, as source of progress and bulwark against sclerosis of the State .... It is the condition *sine qua non* of authentic and lasting progress. This does not mean that the scribe's function ought, by nature, to be oppositional or critical.

En route to this formulation, touching Cameroon specifically, Fame Ndongo praised Biya for "l'ouverture démocratique" in Cameroon since his accession in 1982. He also engaged the central tension Bjornson identified between Ruben um Nyobe and Ahidjo as polar models in Cameroon since independence by dismissing Mongo Beti's 1986 *Lettre ouverte aux Camerounais, ou, La deuxième mort de Ruben um Nyobe,* which transposed Ruben's struggle to his own with Biya's autocracy, as "la manifestation d'une certaine paranoia" (Fame Ndongo 186, 316; see also Breitinger 561).

Mendo Ze, trained like Fame Ndongo but a less prolific writer, appeared once in *Abbia,* with an article on Césaire in 1979; the contrast with Towa's 1969 essay and its political thrust was notable, and revealing. In Césaire's *Cahier d'un retour au pays natal,* Mendo Ze found "un hermétisme déroutant/a baffling hermeticism" where "[l]a syntaxe et la morphologie obéissent a une logique très embarrassante" (34-37: 257) 'syntax and morphology obey a quite awkward logic.' Over 22 pages were scattered word counts, structural analyses, in short a reductive "décodage" leading to the question:

> Trente-neuf ans plus tard c'est-a-dire dans une Afrique presque entièrement independante, à qui s'adresse un ouvrage comme le *Cahier* ... ?

> Twenty-nine years later, that is, in an Africa that is almost entirely independent, to whom is a work like the *Cahier* addressed?

with an answer which returned to what he found in Césaire to be "hermétique .. . à la fois réel et symbolique ... dans cet ouvrage d'un retour de soi a soi et pour soi" (34-37: 277-278) 'hermetic ... both real and symbolic ... in this work of a return of the self to the self and for the self.' The point here is not which of the two is correct on Césaire; what matters is the contrast between Towa's 1969 use of the poet's historical and political experience and sensibility against Mendo Ze's 1979 probe of style and symbol, the interior world of the text, as

107

evidence of *Abbia's* scholarly focus and reflection of Cameroon at large in the journal's latter stages. This may be an example of what moved Bjornson, with all his regard for Fonlon, to judge that *Abbia* "no longer served as an important forum for the exchange of ideas" in its last years (303). As, for Mendo Ze (may one say "de soi à soi pour soi"?), he moved in the late 1980s to the director's post of the still, in 1995, fully monopolistic government radio and television service, CRTV.

So we have Njoh-Mouelle, Fame Ndongo, Mendo Ze as theorists and practitioners of Biya's étatist political culture. We can add the scholar-ministers Joseph Owona and Augustin Kontchou Kouomegni as more powerful legalists to the list of those in letters, with ferocious regime credentials and wealth which took visible form in 1995 as the former celebrated his new CFA billionaire status and the latter constructed a vast estate near the Bamenda-Douala-Yaounde road junction at his native Baham. And to dispel the impression that this is solely a matter of Cameroon francophones trained in France, we can also add the younger anglophone Peter Agbor Tabi, with a PhD from the USA and simultaneously in 1995 Rector of University of Yaounde I, Cameroon's first and still largest campus, and Minister of Higher Education. Their view of the connection between knowledge and power through office and wealth, their collective sense of vigilance, are not Fonlon's, their writing and advocacy are not like *Abbia's* at its inception. Their emergence fits the trajectory Biya chose in 1984 when he proclaimed the "Republic of Cameroon" succeeding the Federal and United Republic eras, erasing all traces of the pluralist origins which were so much *Abbia's* pride and central political culture in its best years.

IV. *Abbia:* Its Legacy and Future Bearings in Cameroon

Abbia ceased publication in 1982, Biya's first year in the presidency when he insisted it be brought into the Ministry of Information and Culture. The editorial board refused, and its subventions ceased (Asanga interview). If it had continued instead under Biya, directed by his own and his intelligentsia's rhetorically reformist but largely discredited "Renewal/New Deal/Communal Liberalism" of the 1980s and "Advanced Democracy" claims of the 1990s, could *Abbia* have resisted the pressures revealed here, even had Fonlon, patriotic but indefatigably Socratic, remained? Had it survived, would it be in the vanguard of criticism that, as we document below, burst forth in 1990? The evidence here, even without the state's pressure, suggests the exhaustion that ventures like *Abbia* encounter in circumstances like Cameroon's, the difficulty in passing its torch/bâton, and the possibility that its honorable past is just that, no less but no more.

Very little so far in this study refutes Bayart in its introduction, regarding the African intelligentsia's failure to arm civil society, conceptually, against the state. Cameroon's early vanguard intellectuals created in *Abbia* a culture of criticism, not a politics of resistance. Fonlon in 1972, the key year when Ahidjo's referendum centralized Cameroon's state, in a key passage cited earlier but now more pointedly, declared the genuine intellectual's commitment "to be the Conscience and not merely the Agent of *society*" rather than of the state (26: 30-33; emphasis added).

That is the gap and failure Bayart discerned. Cameroon's state thereafter proved largely unaccountable. As we saw, many of Fonlon's potential successors chose through the 1980s to remain in or join the regime under Biya, although some defiant colloquia, publications and newspapers like *Le Messager* kept the critical faith. Indeed, the verdict on *Abbia's* remarkable director himself must ultimately include his compliant politics while a minister as well as his defiant culture, a certain Platonism in his view of state leadership beside the Socratic dissent registered above from *Abbia,* and his

109

choice to remain, although inactive, on the ruling party's central committee until his sudden death while in Canada in 1986. It is hardly conceivable he would have remained even nominally a regime party man had he lived until 26 May 1990, when his fellow anglophone from North West Province, John Fru Ndi, launched the opposition Social Democratic Front in Bamenda, resulting in security force's gunfire which killed six young civilians. In any event, a full and critical Fonlon study would now be timely, to assess his legacy by aligning his published and unpublished works with the many eulogies and essays others have issued (Lyonga; Ewumbue Monono; Lantum).

Now, 30+ years after the journal's creation, 10+ years since it ceased, in a quite different Cameroonian political culture which includes the Vichist vocabulary, it should surprise no one if, as part of that legacy in the 1990s, able successors to *Abbia* are now in the works. The periodical *Terroirs: Revue africaine de sciences sociales,* first published in 1992 with Fabien Eboussi Boulaga as editor, is a candidate. So is the newspaper *Le Terroir,* started in 1995 with the purpose "Assumer la culture pour mieux bâtir" 'to take on culture in order to build better' stated immediately below the masthead. Its provenance is especially intriguing, for the publisher is Adamou Ndam Njoya, from the family of the Sultan of Bamum who early in this century created the script, adopted by *Abbia,* noted above as a symbol of indigenous culture at its best. This current prince was a notably forthright Minister of National Education in Ahidjo's last years, has kept a good reputation by avoiding government posts since then, and is in fact the founder and president of a current opposition party, the Cameroon Democratic Union.

Ndam Njoya is a measured critic. But Biya since 1990 faces from more hostile critics a politics of resistance from civil society, including a broad range of intellectuals who survived the 1980s and their followers. They could create a truly resistant culture, not restrained by the kind of ambivalent message transmitted in Eteki Mboumoua's welcome to *Abbia* in 1963, not umbilically tied by office, patronage or other forms of interest and livelihood to the state structure, not by choice or necessity exiled. Towa is not among them.

110

He made his peace with Biya, has long been identified with their mutual Beti ethnic interest which dominates Cameroon's state, and perhaps most ironically of all was named the first rector of the new University of Yaounde II in 1993, though later dismissed. A thorough study of him, as of Fonlon, would illuminate the links between knowledge and power addressed here.

But other elders from the culture and politics of *Abbia*'s and Ahidjo's time have surfaced in the current opposition. The dissident Melone's exile abroad and subsequent village isolation ended with National Assembly membership in the decade before his death 27 June 1995. He at least fitfully challenged the regime, first in a critical wing of Biya's party, then in one remnant of Ruben um Nyobe's party, the Union des Populations du Cameroun; an appalling revenge made Joseph Owona the state's representative at his funeral.

Most remarkable, though, is the transformation of the consummate establishment figure François Sengat Kuo. A poet and *Présence Africaine* editorial associate in the 1950s, we have not yet included him here because he never appeared in *Abbia*. But his loyalties were clear. Bjornson identified Sengat Kuo as the central cultural spokesman in Ahidjo's mature and Biya's early years (189, 286). He served their parties and presidencies; to accentuate an earlier point, he was Biya's Minister of Information and Culture. More than a "fonctionnaire," he was *the* careerist intellectual for 25 years, linked fundamentally with both regimes as a key source on his own admission of constitutional realignments toward presidential autocracy, and, many believe, as the major source of Biya's 1987 reformist tract, *Communal Liberalism.* Yet Sengat Kuo in 1991 organized the most fundamental dissent within his party, then resigned and became a political ally of and close advisor to Biya's major challenger, Fru Ndi, who in all likelihood won the 1992 presidential election but was thwarted by Biya's successful maneuvers to retain office.

More salient by far, *younger* critics continue to emerge. Beginning in 1990 and widely published in Cameroon's independent press as well as in scholarly circles, the dissident Mongo Beti scholar

111

Ambroise Kom's writings flayed the "organic intellectuals" engaged in regime panegyric and the "mythification of power." He singled out Fame Ndongo for applying his semiotic theory by orchestrating a "communication-spectacle" style which the ruling party mobilized against dissent on its emergence in 1990 (Kom 22/1, 87, 89; 22/4, 151). Augmenting this critique in another setting from 1992, Kom became prominent in a series of publications from a Yaounde group, Collectif pour Changer le Cameroun, offering comprehensive blueprints for new structures of politics, economy and society. These and other francophones already at work with *Terroirs* started in 1994 a weekly newspaper, *Génération,* where criticism flourishes in essays by Cameroon-based writers and scholars like Dorothée Kom and Maurice Kamto, and by colleagues like Achille Mbembe and Célestin Monga working abroad. There is also from these ranks the striking case of the scholar-priest Jean-Marc Ela, who left for Canada in mid-1995, citing persistent threats on his life. Some of these writers appear among Bjornson's dissidents as creative writers, others are from the social and applied sciences; many are simultaneously active in opposition parties and human rights advocacy.

Their anglophone counterparts are less well known in the national intelligentsia, but many of them work more directly with the opposition political parties and their forays in cultural politics cut just as deeply. The dramatists Bole Butake and Bate Besong stand out, both on the stage and in periodic writings for *The Herald* and *Cameroon Post,* the leading opposition English language newspapers. Varied genres of literary production and study in English identify, among others, Babila Mutia in Yaounde (his iconoclastic poem in the last *Abbia* was noted above), Nalova Lyonga in Buea (she was Fonlon's student and *Abbia* associate in its last years, the journal's most substantially placed woman), and Linus Asong and Emmanuel Fru Doh in Bamenda as emerging voices. Now requiring more detailed study as a productive English language community of writers, such people can be expected not only to publish more prolifically as they create their own channels to do so, but also to criticize the regime, perhaps with more determination as a minority than the voice of the francophones (Lyonga, Breitinger, and Butake). This group includes the special case of the literary scholar Siga Asanga, who helped found the Social Democratic Front in 1990 but was expelled in 1995. It is not yet possible to judge his career, but he may be instructive in future, like Fonlon and Towa previously, as a study in the orientation of intellectuals to opposition and the state apparatus, and the uses of both.

There is a price exacted for many such efforts. Kom himself was suspended from the University of Yaounde I in 1994 after returning from a Fulbright award in the USA. A foremost critic of the material decay, politicization, and mediocrity of that campus, the physicist Jongwane Dipoko, formed its first independent teachers' union in 1991. A year later, when the union published bilingually a book with documents, in English *The University in Cameroon: An Institution in Disarray,* he suffered hand wounds in a machete attack, but continues to lead resistance there to the legacy of faults and crimes which he claims the Rector-Minister, Agbor Tabi, makes worse. Patrice Ndedi Penda in Douala, dating back a quarter century as one of Bjornson's prime writer-critic examples of dissent, constantly dodges censors, lawsuits and bankruptcy with his newspaper *Galaxie.* It has appeared under four separate titles to evade prosecution since 1990, and five consecutive issues in mid-1995 were seized from kiosks, *Galaxie* thus both incurring the costs of printing and losing the revenue of sales. From this evidence, one wonders what faces another intellectual-turned-critic and activist, Tazoacha Asonganyi, of Yaounde's medical faculty, following his assumption of the Secretary General's post in the Social Democratic Front succeeding Asanga, next in party rank to Fru Ndi.

To summarize and conclude a mid-1990s perspective for this study, the state's most prominent critic, target and victim among the intelligentsia is now Mongo Beti. Non-resident in Cameroon since 1951 and never a visitor since 1959, he resumed brief visits as opposition pressure forced some political windows open in 1991, with a hostile reception (Breitinger 567-71, through 1991). He committed to stay in 1993, very much in the resistance vanguard. In

113

quick succession, he declared and demonstrated support for Fru Ndi's Social Democratic Front, delivered in *La France contre l'Afrique: Retour au Cameroun* another broadside against neocolonialism, opened Librairie des Peuples Noirs as an oppositionist Yaounde bookstore, and blasted the regime in *Génération* and other newspapers with reports about the current misery of his natal village as well as broader commentaries. On 4 February 1995, for refusing to stand aside and defer to a presidential cavalcade speeding between Yaounde's city center and airport (for another of Biya's French visits he detests), Beti at age 65 was beaten badly enough to require treatment in hospital. Yaounde authorities routinely deny permits to or simply break up his book promotions and political appearances.

As the analysis concludes on these notes of challenges and reprisals to mid-1995, there is composite evidence, both systematic and anecdotal, of determined resistance by the generation following those who framed independent Cameroon's early national political culture in *Abbia*. Does Biya, himself a "fonctionnaire" in Melone's sense, facing the Vichist charge behind these initiatives, recall the *Abbia* phase of his own apprenticeship 30 years ago? Cameroon's youth and young adults in the 1990s are not without guidance from the legacy of *Abbia* that its survivors and successors among the intelligentsia now shape. Whether or not it is a conscious model, it surely has useful potential. It will be especially interesting to see whether Fonlon's original bilingual aspirations for Cameroon, however modified in his last years, can still provide present and future voices a bridge. The steady growth of anglophone federalist, sovereigntist, even secessionist politics makes this questionable, and the publications since 1990 which could succeed *Abbia* are more the products of only one language community than *Abbia* was. One also wonders how and where Fonlon would direct his "anathema" text of 1982 in Cameroon's politics of the 1990s.

Such issues and questions remain, but in no way diminish the sense that a new, quite different dispensation in culture, as in politics, is possible, and could help establish the conditions necessary to satisfy a later part of Bayart's article that introduced this study, and now provides its fitting last words:

> There are many reasons for being pessimistic over the outcome of these conflicts. Nevertheless, we shall not underestimate a society's capacity to 'invent democracy.' (qtd. in Chabal 124)

Acknowledgments

I am most grateful to the Archbishop of Bamenda, Paul Verdzekov, for access to the complete run of *Abbia* in the cathedral library, and to Ambroise Kom for sending materials from Cameroon and reviewing first and last drafts of this text. Among Richard Bjornson's last courtesies was advice on this project. Two members of the Bernard Fonlon Society, Kevin Mbayu in Yaounde and Dr. Guillaume Penda Etongue in Douala, encouraged the work. Research leaves from Western Washington University funded the analysis of *Abbia* and interviews in Cameroon during 1989 and 1991, then the search for subsequent evidence during 1995. An earlier version of the paper was presented at the 1992 meeting of the African Studies Association in Seattle.

Works Cited

Abbia: Cameroon Cultural Review. 1963-82.

Arnold, Stephen. "An Interview about Literature with Bernard Fonlon." *World Literature Written in English* 20.1 (1981): 48-62.

Bayart, Jean-François "Civil Society in Africa." *Political Domination in Africa.* Ed. Patrick Chabal. Cambridge: Cambridge UP, 1986. 109-25.

Bjornson, Richard. *The African Quest for Freedom and Identity: Cameroonian Writing and the National Experience.* Bloomington: Indiana UP, 1991.

Breitinger, Eckhard. "'Lamentations Patriotiques': Writers, Censors and Politics in Cameroon." *African Affairs* 92.369 (1993): 557-75.

Ewumbue Monono, Churchill. *The Torch and the Throne: The Political Philosophy of Bernard Fonlon.* Yaounde: SOPECAM, 1991.

Fame Ndongo, Jacques. *Le Prince et le scribe.* Paris: Berger-Levrault, 1988.

Kom, Ambroise. "Writing Under A Monocracy." Research *in African Literatures* 22/1 (1991): 83-92.

___ . "Mongo Beti Returns to Cameroon: Journey to the End of the Night." *Research in African Literatures* 22.4 (1991): 47-53.

Lantum, Daniel. *Dr. Bernard Nsokika Fonlon: An Intellectual in Politics.* Yaounde: SOPECAM, 1992.

Lyonga, Nalova. *Socrates in Cameroon.* Yaounde: Tortoise, 1989.

___ , Eckhard Breitinger and Bole Butake. *Anglophone Cameroon Writing.* Bayreuth: Bayreuth African Studies *30/WEKA-A Journal of Anglophone Cameroon Writing and the Arts* 1, 1993.

Varied sources in Cameroon, principally interviews in 1989 with Eldridge Mohammadou and Dr. Marcien Towa, and in 1991 with William Eteki Mboumoua, then in 1995 the newspapers *Génération, La Nouvelle Expression, Le Messager,* January-July, and an interview with Dr. Siga Asanga.

Despite what I wrote late in the 1996 text, and Fabien Eboussi Boulaga's efforts with *Terroirs, Revue africaine de sciences socials et de philosophie*, no journal equaling *Abbia* has appeared since its last issue. Its legacy is difficult to find in Cameroon three decades later, save for the independent journalism of *Le Messager* and its counterparts, which the 2010 death of *Le Messager's* founder Pius Njawe collectively diminished. For a compressed version of *Abbia*'s story in a more global framework, interested readers can consult my chapter entitled "The formative journals and institutions" in *The Cambridge History of African and Caribbean Literature* (2004), volume 1, pp. 398-407.

All this now verges on old history. Is there, anywhere in Cameroon today, a Phoenix preparing to rise from *Abbia*'s ashes?

Chapter 3

Politics erupts

A drastic change in Cameroon's circumstances took place between 1989 and my next research visit there, 1991, which accounts for my own transformation, as if by catapult, from a scholar of recent culture, education, language and development into an historian of contemporary political dynamics and especially of the opposition Social Democratic Front (SDF) party.

There was reason to wonder, months before that second sojourn began, 24 June 1991, whether it would follow the original design to complete work on the *Abbia* text and to plot how to turn the 1989 reconnaissance into a book along July's and Bjornson's scholarly paths. News from Judy, already conducting research there since early 1991, alerted me to a very different Cameroon than 1989's, especially in Bamenda, since the SDF's birth there in the blood of six demonstrators shot to death as its inaugural rally dispersed, 26 May 1990, and the creation and spread of an opposition politics.

Reading about Cameroon during my eighteen month absence, and speculating on the impact of democratization impulses elsewhere like the Iron Curtain's collapse, Nelson Mandela's freedom and Sam Nujoma's Namibia presidency, was one thing. Quite another was Judy's cumulative account toward mid-1991 of a Monday-Friday general strike in Bamenda, non-violent but strictly enforced by the SDF and its partners in opposition, which the Cameroon state could not contain. It had closed all public functions there except schools, health facilities and petty street trade in essentials, and was spreading to other cities under the rubric "villes mortes/ghost town." Students were returning from the University of Yaounde campus, rebutting the "zéro mort" official version of April-May demonstrations there and joining their more generic grievances to local challenges across the range of governance. New conditions, like the absence of taxis to

119

use for her research access to villages beyond Bamenda, registered in Judy's unplanned but necessary purchase of a veteran Volkswagen from the Catholic archdiocese. Both met me in Douala June 24 and the car's display of a palm frond, the opposition emblem, was the safeguard for our drive north to Bamenda, which began with our view of one notable sign of the now hyper-volatile politics, the ashen remains of Lapiro de Mbanga's nightclub on Douala's outskirts.

These and other early to mid-1991 circumstances framed "la crise/the crisis" brewing in Cameroon. Biya's June 27 radio address to the nation gave it high definition, rejecting as "sans objet" a sovereign national conference that opposition forces demanded, citing Benin, Mali and Togo precedents. Defiant response was swift. Bamenda's people mounted roadblocks against routine traffic, and ever larger Monday, Wednesday and Friday street demonstrations in the 10,000 size range became immediate "order of the day" oppositional routines. These actions brought reinforced security personnel, with street sweeps, helicopter patrols, tear gas, concussion grenades and bullets. Injuries and occasional fatalities recurred, as government forces and a fundamentally non-armed, non-violent opposition contested the city.

Who from the 1960s could be oblivious to these surroundings? Although my reading of *Abbia* continued and neared its completion, and I was accredited to and attended the Bamenda and Yaounde sessions of the ministry-led Etats-Généraux on culture that fed my original research scheme (more than 1989's on education, which I studied only second hand), my interests veered towards politics. I soon began what turned into the paper reproduced just below in the form it reached by 1994.

The original intent was not so much academic as directly informational, more journalistic than historical. It was my good fortune to be, as far as I've ever learned, the sole research scholar with history and politics bearings who was in Bamenda throughout mid- to late 1991, at a time when the government was at pains to mute or deny what was happening there. Information was difficult to circulate. Cameroon's independent newspapers carried Bamenda material, but their resources were limited and they had to skirt both pre-publication censorship and post-publication confiscations. Risk-taking Cameroonians like Boh Herbert and his counterparts challenged "official" reports in print and in early electronic forms for both domestic and overseas audiences, but the city's roughly 400 kilometer distance from Yaounde shielded its mounting tensions from potentially interested parties like foreign embassies and non-governmental organizations in the capital that, a year after the SDF's formation, still deemed Bamenda peripheral. Save for "stringer" journalists and a brief mid-September 1991 visit by the U.S.A.'s National Democratic Institute, which sharply criticized state policy and actions in a 1992 report, few non-Cameroonians both knew of and documented the city's centrality to the emerging struggle.

Recognizing an opportunity to track events that mattered, perceiving a compressed, Yaounde-Bamenda version of a "two solitudes" life in crisis time, I observed opposition protocols from the time I arrived. They taught me "on the ground" conditions, from early morning walks down Station Hill's bush paths alongside adults and children with essential provision head loads, regular attendance at Monday-Wednesday-Friday opposition rallies, SDF contacts at a Ghana Street off-licence, and afternoon climbs up Station Hill's tarred road to our house. These treks led me into and past the protests staged between Finance Junction and the Senior Divisional Officer's headquarters, which revealed Bamenda's own "two solitudes" separation between civil society in the city's valley and the government installations "Up Station." One key diagnostic episode along that roadway stood out: the periodic demonstrations by senior female title society members to support the resistance, including disrobings that threw security forces into disarray (with a "we are your mothers!" message among others) in an updated version of the cycle of *anlu* protests around 1960 identified in Paul Nkwi's and Eugenia Shanklin's writings. This chapter's reprinted text missed the full significance of this 1990s *takumbeng* experience that Susan Diduk and (with collaborators) Charles Fonchingong have since amplified, but my later writings made some amends.

These movements and our hilltop house and short walks nearby gave me clear views of opposition actions and security force deployments, anticipative and retaliatory, across Bamenda's urban core and its outliers. That included the near calamity of October 2 when (by my estimate, decently attuned after three months) 50,000 unarmed demonstrators surged toward a small but armed security contingent near the entrance to Nkwen Market. Either by order or default (I never learned which), government weapons were lowered there at noon but they were used later in the day at Mile Three above Nkwen. Amnesty International, *Jeune Afrique Economie* and British Broadcasting Corporation television acquired and circulated evidence of October 2's Bamenda clashes and casualties from participants and observers, and disseminated the first public, widely available evidence abroad about the militant democracy struggle taking place in parts of Cameroon's hinterland.

This ground was not entirely unfamiliar. My doctoral dissertation had covered mid-15th century England's civil wars, with special attention to local episodes of violence, 1430-1450, a time of disruptive social change, discredited governance, and familial power struggles with national consequences (the word "baron" was used then, as in Cameroon in 1991, to designate both "loyalists" within ruling circles and local rivals competing for political power). The upshot in 1450, in the peasant revolt/jacquerie tradition, was Jack Cade's "Rising" that advanced on and paralyzed London before its violent suppression. I could extrapolate from my earlier study, recognize the repudiation of the state in the general strike and insurrection in 1991, and assimilate and query what I now observed and experienced in Cameroon. In fact, my July-August 1991 field notes include conversations I heard about (unlike England in 1450) non-violent plans for opposition treks from both Douala and the Bamenda-Mbouda corridor to converge on and isolate the capital city from the coast and part of the hinterland (a siege) and for a blockade against food transport from those areas to Yaounde ("starve the beast!"), and also for dealing with the violent intervention of security forces that would certainly follow such actions. What oppositional forces were at work? Could governance by (Le Vine's term) "presidential monarchy" based in Yaounde be a target like Henry VI's (mis)rule in London earlier? What was the likely outcome, factoring in fault lines both between and within the contending parties? So the section dated 1991 in "Cameroon's Democratic Crossroads, 1990-4," *The Journal of Modern African Studies*, 32, 4 (1994), pp. 605-628, reproduced just below, "wrote itself" as much as anything in my scholarly experience, as eye-witness Bamenda journalism, reinforced by abundant local print and oral materials, and brief travels elsewhere.

The text took preliminary, decidedly and appropriately Bamenda-centric shape by our December 1991 return home, from which point subsequent events and the more reflective historian in me joined the reflexive journalist, leading to the extended version published in 1994. In that 1991-1994 interval came a legislative election that almost seated an opposition majority, then a presidential ballot and the CPDM's and Biya's flawed and fraudulent defeat of the SDF and its candidate John Fru Ndi late in 1992. The subsequent two month state of emergency imposed on Bamenda and other insurrectionary areas was much less bloody than England's 1450 "restoration of order" but comparable in results. That sequence of events placing the state's resumed presence alongside my 1991 Bamenda experience, when the state had been more reactive than proactive, built a larger "realpolitik" factor into the further research and writing that led to the 1994 text. I trust readers will find some convergence, and balance, between both the text's journalistic and historical bearings and its oppositional and governmental coverage, as the long incipient but now more seasoned Africanist in me took primary shape, then and forward, as an historian of contemporary Cameroon.

Cameroon's Democratic Crossroads, 1990-4

CAMEROON'S upheavals since 1990 have not been widely reported among the more visible and violent African state-society conflicts. Their anonymity on the continent's political agenda is understandable, since by the formal, most visible indices, little has changed since pluralist pressures appeared. The 'Gaullist' monolith state remains fundamentally in place after 25 years: the constitution retains the unitary executive stamp of 1972, against federalist and devolution challenges, although multi-party politics were legalised in 1990. This and a new press law have been the regime's major concessions to emerging opposition forces, and led to presidential and national assembly elections in 1992.

Power and basic initiatives still belong to President Paul Biya and the Cameroon People's Democratic Movement (CPDM), following claims to electoral victories that are still disputed to this day. Despite fierce challenges and shrinking resources, the regime's incumbency, control of the electoral process, monopoly of non-print media, and (ultimately) command of the security apparatus, keep Cameroon confined to the margins of current Africanist coverage of state, civil society, and democratisation issues.

But as this article will show, Cameroonians are far more active as democratic protagonists than any scrutiny of merely institutional politics since 1990 might suggest. Several hundred deaths have resulted from clashes between a precarious regime and a determined citizenry. Despite institutional blockages, resistance continues to develop. The state, though formally intact, drifts, and faces a wide range of challenges from the wider community to (in the generic phrase of the independent press which voices and sustains the opposition) 'le pouvoir/the power'. In short, Cameroon is a crucial example of Africa's tantalising process of democratisation.

Background

Crises in economy and polity have frayed societal bonds in Cameroon since the mid-1980s. The *banyan*-like contours of their domestic roots and foreign branches are broadly understood.[71] For all their authoritarianism and selective repression, President Ahmadu Ahidjo and the Cameroon National Union (CNU) demonstrated until 1982 both negotiating skills with local elites and (in every sense) marketing skills abroad. They sustained steady, even (with petroleum's help) buoyant growth in the economy, and sufficient patterns of opportunity in the patronage distribution of their domestic proceeds. There was enough for many Cameroonians to aspire to, if not to attain. The structure, however, began to decay soon after Ahidjo resigned as President in 1982. His successor, Biya, generally credited with early reformist inclinations, faced a major threat to his regime when northerners who wanted to direct Ahidjo's legacy, apparently with his support, attempted a coup in 1984. It failed, but prompted in its aftermath a reconstruction of the delicately balanced patronage network.

Biya replaced Ahidjo's CNU with his own CPDM in 1985. Formerly predictable regime adjustments among 'barons' soon became matters of competition, speculation, and risk when Cameroon's terms of trade and fiscal arrangements soured. The official economy shrank and brisk foreign participation gave way to International Monetary Fund (IMF)-World Bank caution and conditions. The state's offices and treasury ceased to provide orderly, profitable circuits for the well- connected, opportunistic patrons and clients. Pay-offs yielded to rip-offs as public goods and services, above all parastatals, became targets which the literature on African 'neo-patrimonialism' and 'prebends' now broadly identifies for domestic bandits. Nantang Jua and Nicolas van de Walle have documented the economy's downturn, as well as the subsequent strategy of plunder and its scale. Ahidjo's 'enrichissez-vous' message a quarter century ago has given way to the aphorism often used for elites in now distressed regimes: 'après moi le déluge'.[72]

125

Biya's problems with inter-elite competition for shrinking resources intensified by 1990, when his own Beti ethnic affiliates in and near the capital Yaounde -less than 10 per cent of Cameroon's people, but politically dominant in three of its ten provinces (Centre, South, East) - were identified as the ever more exclusive beneficiaries of the state's remaining largesse. Ahidjo's system, by contrast, had been inclusive, incorporating all elites: his own northerners spanning (what are now) three provinces (Far North, North, Adamaoua); the Bamileke ethnics, whose core population and diaspora were influential in two provinces (West, Littoral), as well as the latter's indigenous Bassa and Duala; and the anglophones in the remaining two provinces (North West, South West), where powers reserved in the 1961 Federation were removed by the 1972 referendum creating a unitary state. Biya, however, more likely captive than *capo,* was yoked to civilian and military Beti leaders who moved beyond conventional patrimonial politics to, in Jua's term, 'ethno-clientelism'. Economic frustration outside their own narrow ranks became anti-Beti ethnic rage. The economic consequences of these shifts spread beyond dependent, marginalised primary producers, petty traders, and workers, subject to state discipline, when pay arrears mounted among civil servants and teachers who could fashion political dissent. The downward spiral left the remnant profiteers exposed for all to see, envy, judge.

Cameroon remained quiet during 1989. But the ingredients for a visible and fundamental crisis, challenging elite management's capacity to absorb or control, were in place. Simultaneously, the upheavals in Eastern and Central Europe were perhaps not a necessary, certainly not a sufficient, but still a precipitating condition for confrontations in Africa at large. They showed the vulnerability of one-party states, and the hesitancy or failure of army intervention in regime crises. Historically sweeping reckonings and retributions surfaced, with populist resolutions thinkable, even demonstrable, at least in the short-term. Nelson Mandela's release from prison and Sam Nujoma's presidential accession early in 1990 added Southern

Africa to the arenas where substantial change encouraged democratic forces.

MAP 1
Cameroon's Cities, Towns, and Provinces since 1983

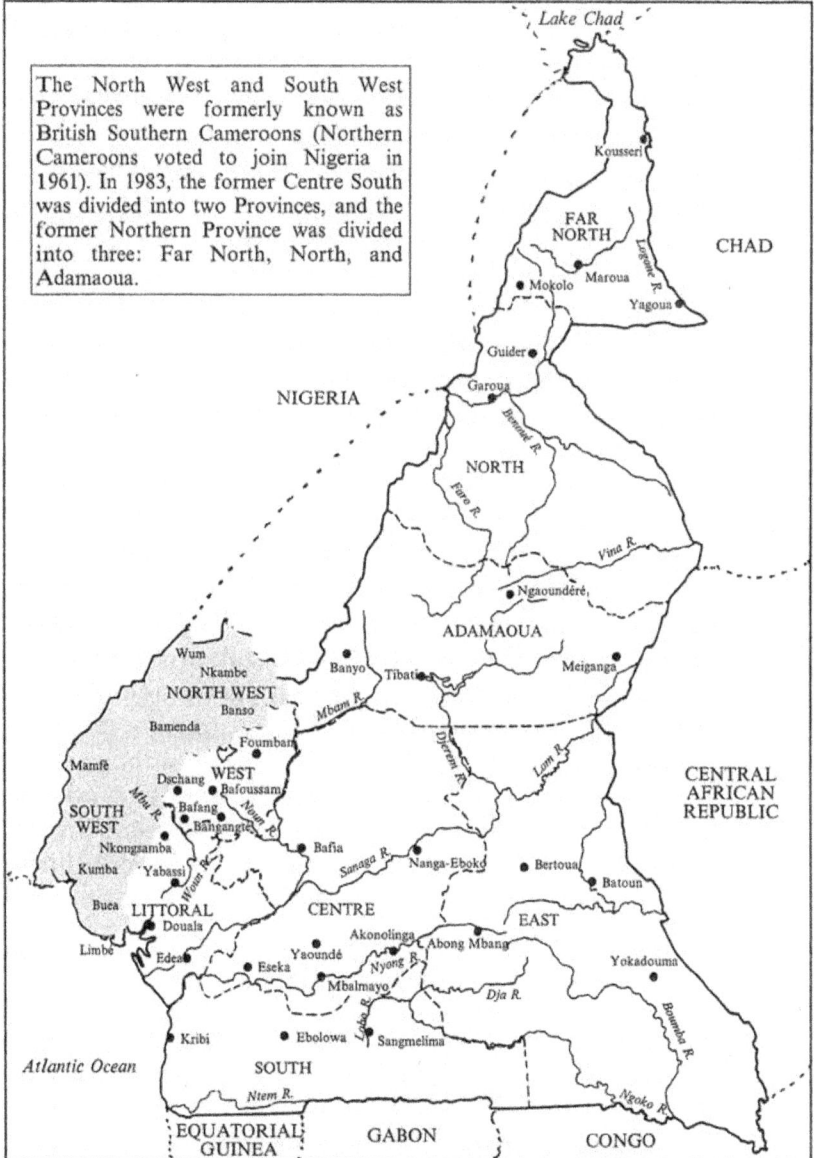

The North West and South West Provinces were formerly known as British Southern Cameroons (Northern Cameroons voted to join Nigeria in 1961). In 1983, the former Centre South was divided into two Provinces, and the former Northern Province was divided into three: Far North, North, and Adamaoua.

1990: Opposition Challenge and Regime Response

Cameroon's crisis began with two arrests early in 1990: first in January when its most contentious journalist, Pius Njawe, the editor of *Le Messager* (Douala), published text about corruption near the Presidency deemed too critical; then in February when Yondo Black, a prominent barrister, tried to form an independent political party. Their trials, convictions, and modest punishments mobilised professional colleagues and publicised the growing dissent, but response was confined within 'la Classe dirigeante'. Nor was there anything obviously explosive in the March 1990 call by an anglophone Bamenda bookshop proprietor, John Fru Ndi, for a new party, the Social Democratic Front (SDF). He had been as recently as 1988 a parliamentary candidate for Biya's CPDM and held a government contract to supply schools.

But a SDF rally in Bamenda in May 1990 proved the incendiary spark. Most likely so as to appear decisive, calculating little risk in a show of force against Cameroon's 25 per cent minority anglophones, the Government reinforced its Bamenda troops. The rally was massive, probably 20,000 strong in a 150,000 population, but peaceful by all accounts except the regime's. As it dispersed, six young Cameroonians were shot dead. Perceived locally as a martyrdom, their deaths created the first national surge of popular outrage. The obscure Fru Ndi became the resistance leader 'Ni John'. A more volatile, open-textured 'movement' in politics meshed with fiscal frustration and ethnic envy. Like South Africa after Soweto, Cameroon was hardly to know a tranquil day thereafter, and the phrase 'la crise/the crisis' has routinely encoded the country's experience for its people ever since.

The atmosphere for the rest of 1990 was charged yet ill-defined, and Cameroon's World Cup football success muted politics. Many of Biya's potential challengers were abroad by choice or in exile. The movement to African soil (notably in Benin and Mali) of democratic openings through national conferences and embryonic electoral politics gave dissenting leadership and public opinion a 'wait and see'

128

option. Caution was reinforced by speculation about how Cameroon's foreign creditors and donors would react to initiatives for change: would Biya and the CPDM be reinforced, nudged towards concessions, or forced to substantial reconstruction of governance?

Not all opposition forces marked time. Fru Ndi and the SDF mobilised anglophone support, and independent weekly newspapers appeared in the key southern francophone cities, Yaounde, Douala, and Bafoussam, on largely Bamileke funding. Previously subdued voices became public; the regime, its agencies, and its personnel faced savage critiques. Witness such cutting references as 'Popaul' for Biya, and the popular play of acronyms widespread by late 1990: the CPDM's 'Chop People Dem Moni', in Pidgin, loosely paraphrased, 'They eat our money like it's their own'; and the Cameroon Radio and Television (CRTV)'s alleged 'Centre de Rééstablissement Total de Voleurs/Centre for the Complete Resettlement of Thieves. Biya suffered ridicule as a 'small boy' in the shadow of Ahidjo, the erstwhile 'big man' whose reputation enjoyed an oddly favourable afterglow in this, the year following his death in exile, and Biya's refusal of the customary, honourable burial in Cameroon (which may alone have produced a popular critical idiom against Biya in the otherwise still silent 'Great North').

As yet scattered, still relying more on CPDM blunders than on their own strength, human rights and political party forces kept exerting pressure on the President to reform policies and institutions (and Biya is likely to have been receiving similar foreign 'advice'). The regime's first bench mark response came in December 1990, when the National Assembly legalised the year's two *faits accomplis,* party and press pluralism. The state retained the will and residual capacity for *ad hoc* repression, but the opposition was ready and able to move in 1991 from persuasion to organisation, from words to acts. Cameroon's politics now decisively broke elite ranks; the established vocabulary and emerging practice of democratisation opened avenues for direct action.

129

1991: Party Formations, Alliances, and Confrontations

Political parties began to multiply from early 1991. The Union des Populations du Cameroun (UPC), historically the base of militant resistance, was reinstated from outlawry, while others, like the SDF, were newly recognised or created. More newspapers started to circulate, challenging the official media and thereby becoming increasingly popular -- according to a report from Paris, Njawe's *Le Messager* was printing as many copies each week as were sold by the government's daily *Cameroon Tribune* (Yaounde).[73] By mid-year there were more than 50 parties and papers in the field. Many of the new organisations were ephemeral, and some either proclaimed or disguised a regime provenance, but the mobilisation and contest of fresh opinion and resources were palpable. As exiles returned, political debate echoed past and voiced new grievances.

The new journalism spread the war of words launched by political parties, interest groups, human rights organisations, and other voluntary associations. Opposition tapped deep into the populations of major southern and western cities, and began to engage the streets. One clash in particular, during April, raised the stakes and the level of violence, when security forces turned on student demonstrators at the University of Yaounde. This act was meant, like that taken at Bamenda the year before, to teach those involved a lesson, in this case a restive student body (triple the size of the planned campus limits), warning it against any linkage with the parties or Yaounde's populace. Against government claims on the spot and a later commission of enquiry's report that none were killed, the opposition named six dead victims and claimed many more. This intensified allegations of regime brutality' and added 'Zéro Mort' to the resistance lexicon of rage and ridicule.

By June the major opposition parties had adopted the now common francophone African demand for a sovereign *Conférence nationale* to supersede presidential one-party rule, and were calling for civil disobedience in forms like tax refusal until it was convened. Biya's response to the National Assembly, live on radio and television

130

to a gathered nation, the regime's second bench-mark for the mounting crisis, came on 27 June: 'Je l'ai dit et je le maintiens, la Conférence nationale est sans objet pour le Cameroun/ I have said it and repeat it, the National Conference has no purpose for Cameroon'. Within minutes barricades rose and tires burned in the streets of Douala. By nightfall one gendarme and three civilians were dead in this historically radical city, which now gave Bamenda an opposition vanguard partner among francophones. 'Sans Objet' joined 'Zéro Mort' as a slogan for resistance which, far more than Biya's message, 'went national'.

From 5 July 'Monsieur Sans Objet' faced a general strike in and around Douala, Bamenda, Bafoussam, and most other large cities in four southern and western provinces.[74] It held firm in all these places through September, and lasted until Christmas in Bamenda and Bafoussam. Douala's port, handling 80 + per cent of the foreign trade of both Cameroon and its smaller neighbours, shut down. Inter- and intra-city public and private transport, shops, stalls, and curbside markets closed Monday to Friday. Banks dispensing civil service pay, among their other functions, opened only intermittently on Saturdays, depending on a cash flow steadily reduced by capital flight abroad and withdrawal of funds from the domestic economy. Reprisals by militants threatened strike breakers, and massive demonstrations maintained strike solidarity. Bamenda's three rallies per week during the second half of 1991 never drew less than 8,000-10,000 people, and mustered up to 50,000 for especially defiant days like 2 October, when security forces using a helicopter and ground troops left two dead and dozens in hospital (several lost limbs from concussion grenades).[75]

Intense party activity can be summarised in a few essentials. The CPDM elites splintered: Biya loyalists represented an ever more narrow ethnic Beti core in the Centre, South, and East Provinces; dissidents like the senior state and party official, François Sengat Kuo, called for the *Conférence nationale* so as to defuse the crisis or at least buy time; some deserted the CPDM, like the younger, ambitious Douala leader, Jean-Jacques Ekindi, who resigned and formed his

131

own party. While the regime faltered and 'villes mortes/ghost towns' took hold, the opposition's momentum became the most salient feature until September. Frequent 'co-ordination' meetings drew the parties together, and consensus emerged on demands for reduced presidential powers, decentralised national administration, 'accountability' in public services, and liberal-to-social democratic policies with a human- rights focus.

But the co-ordinated strategy for this platform, the national conference, and the strike could not prevent the opposition's fragmentation. Previous regime connections and rivalries compromised its leaders. Returning exiles added more competition than unity. Fru Ndi's SDF spread its influence but remained an anglophone force, and was far more popular in the North West than the South West Province, for language affiliation there did not preclude economic and ethnic rivalry. Adamou Ndam Njoya, an Ahidjo-era minister, and his Cameroon Democratic Union (CDU), relied on his royal familial base in the city and sultanate of Foumban, West Province, and sought support among that area's Bamileke diaspora in major southern cities. Bello Bouba Maigari (Biya's first Vice-President) returned from exile, and his National Union for Democracy and Progress (NUDP) soon dominated the three mostly Muslim northern provinces. The UPC, its leadership hopelessly divided, retained substantial support only in and around Douala. These parties could not turn regional into national followings.

The opposition was also divided by 'bread and butter' issues. Most exemplary was September's debate on whether to add a boycott of the 1991-2 school year in its core areas to the general strike. It was hard to imagine anything more contentious, given such popular faith in the benefits of education, and the concern for loss of revenue which schools generate for middle and lower-class Cameroonians in the service sector, notably transport and food-vending. Here, the opposition's popularity confronted the reality of income choice, individual and household, immediate and long-range, and no ideology or strategy could close the gap. The first truly contested executive vote taken by the SDF narrowly favoured the boycott, but was not broadly effective.[76]

As the consensual base of the opposition weakened and competitive ambitions to succeed Biya played *their* role, regime initiatives resumed. The President made an 'air lift' national tour, mixing unity rhetoric and the waning enticements of incumbency and the national treasury as best he could, also counting on the increasing disarray of those opposed to the CPDM. He then announced in October 1991 that the legislative elections would be held a year earlier than scheduled, in February 1992. This was a tactically shrewd, even decisive move, as newspapers recognised: the official *Cameroon Tribune* proclaimed 'Aux Urnes Citoyens!/Citizens to the Polls!', while the opposition *Challenge Hebdo* (Douala) warned of 'Le Piège/The Trap!'. And so it proved: Biya made his Prime Minister available for 'consultations' with individual opposition parties, promised electoral code and constitutional reforms, and secured the so-called Yaounde Declaration, the agreement reached on 13 November 1991, by 40 of the 47 registered parties, to replace the national conference demand with elections, and to end the strike.

Most significantly for future reference, since it separated them clearly from all others in the viable opposition, Fru Ndi and the SDF refused to sign the Declaration. With the apparent return of 'normalcy' in Cameroon, the general strike ended, the National Assembly met, French financial aid resumed, and the promised elections diluted demands for a national conference. What better proof could there be of the regime's democratic intent? Virtually imprisoned at the presidential palace and his country estate in mid-1991 by the 'Sans Objet' fiasco, Biya now looked and acted safe, travelling both home and abroad. By contrast, the opposition was split and the independent press was full of comments about 'trahison/betrayal'. The elections die was cast and would be the measure of Cameroon's 1992 politics.

1992: Electoral Tests of Strength

More uncertainty than resolution characterised the campaign for the National Assembly elections, postponed but finally held on 1 March 1992. Biya's failure to implement his reform promises caused defections from the Yaounde Declaration,[77] and eventually the poll was boycotted by 35 of the (by now) 69 parties, including the SDF and the CDU. The support received by the regime in their core areas, with low voter turnouts of under 30 per cent, provided the very seats which gave the CPDM, and a partner it had created and financed in the north, a slim majority of 94 members in the 180-member National Assembly.[78]

Bello Bouba's NUDP won 68 of the 86 non-regime seats from eight provinces, and became the only opposition party that was electorally active from the time of the Yaounde Declaration in November 1991 until the National Assembly convened in June 1992 to gain national support. But Fru Ndi and the SDF pressed their claim to the true mantle of popular leadership for (they could, and did, argue) an unwavering and principled rejection of Biya's manipulative politics which had never yet placed in jeopardy or offered alternatives to his regime's mainstays: namely, the unitary state and the executive presidency, as well as the armed forces which ultimately sustained them. These themes dominated the SDF convention in May, which meant that the party was adequately prepared to contend for what still constituted real power in Cameroon when the regime brought forward the date of the presidential poll. By being able to brand much of the opposition as opportunist since late 1991, the SDF was able to lead more reliable allies into a Union for Change coalition in support of Fru Ndi.

This election advanced SDF fortunes. Both Biya and Fru Ndi claimed the Presidency on plurality counts near 40 per cent, leaving 19 per cent for Bello Bouba and the NUDP, in a poll deemed unacceptably flawed by observers from the Washington-based National Democratic Institute for International Affairs. Its report found 'serious fault with the electoral process' which 'simply does not make it possible to determine which candidate received the most votes or which candidate would have been the winner in a fair election'.[79] But even the regime's own data demonstrated that the SDF had made gains both in CPDM and other opposition party territory.[80] The critical terrain was a cluster of three provinces, constituting a bulge with at least two million people, south and east from the North West base of Fru Ndi. In the South West, Littoral, and West, he polled 52, 68, and 68 per cent, respectively, reversing their NUDP or UPC majorities in the National Assembly elections that the SDF had boycotted seven months before.

Two other salient patterns emerged. The 68 per cent victories for Fru Ndi were in two populous francophone provinces, Littoral and West, which meant that he had bridged part of Cameroon's historical language gulf. Equally significant were his margins of success in the major urban electoral districts of all three of the new support-base provinces, where commerce and industry create cosmopolitan and incipiently class-constituted migrant populations, less marked by 'vertical cleavages' of language and ethnicity: Fako (Limbe city) 77 per cent, Wouri (Douala) 69 per cent, Mifi (Bafoussam) 89 per cent, and Mungo (Nkongsamba) 87 per cent. In the 15 *départements* in these three provinces, Fru Ndi won with majorities in eight and pluralities in two. Perhaps most startling elsewhere was the fact that he received as much as 39 per cent of the votes cast at the regime's epicentre, Mfoundi (Yaounde), as against 52 per cent for Biya. By contrast, Fru Ndi failed in the three northern Muslim provinces, where the NUDP held its ground, as well as the pro-CPDM East, South, and Centre provinces (outside Yaounde) ; he won 10 per cent of the poll in just four of their *30 départemenis.*

The regime continued in power by using a compliant Supreme Court to certify its victory, by press censorship, and by a formal state of emergency which shackled the SDF and kept Fru Ndi on his Bamenda compound until it was lifted at the end of 1992. But the presidential poll fundamentally altered Cameroon's politics, in part because rural bias favoured the regime less than in the legislative

135

elections, but far more because the SDF's momentum was clearly a very important new development.

1993-4: Uneasy Truce, Unresolved Crisis

The NUDP's parliamentary base and the SDF's presidential poll in 1992 created, alongside the CPDM, a three-way political party dynamic for 1993. Only three of the dozens of other parties which operated during 1991-2 retained pockets of allegiance. The CPDM's cat's-paw ally with six legislative seats, the Movement for the Defence of the Republic (MDR), was its agent among non-Muslims in the Far North; its leader, Dakole Diassala, had a cabinet post but no obvious wider electoral potential. The CDU kept active only near Foumban; Ndam Njoya had been a potential leader of an opposition coalition before signing the Yaounde Declaration, thereby losing any wider popular mandate. The UPC tapped residual ties in the Littoral Province, especially among the Bassa, but its leadership was so contested and discredited as to threaten its existence after half a century of vanguard resistance to the French and all successor regimes. After electing 10 per cent of the legislators early in 1992, it basically defaulted during the ensuing presidential vote.

In the three-party mainstream from early 1993, the CPDM still relied on support in the capitals and hinterlands of the East, South, and Centre Provinces. But the party faced a challenge in Yaounde, and yielded both to the west of its core area before reaching a Douala-Bafoussam axis which marked the SDF advance, and to the north where it was by and large outstripped by the NUDP (and where both dominated the SDF). Biya commanded the remaining patronage and other powers of incumbency, press censorship, television and radio monopolies (the latter dented by 'off shore' transmissions), and of course the state's security forces.

An electoral combination between the SDF and the NUDP at any time since 1991 would have taken control of civilian politics, but it was not yet forged and mutual distrust between these parties increased. [81] Fru Ndi staged a number of rallies before large crowds in Yaounde, where the SDF was harassed but not excluded.[82] Visits to the United States (during the inauguration of President Bill Clinton) and to France and Britain increased his 'visibility' and stature. Bello Bouba and the NUDP remained a force in the north and the legislature, and entered all political calculations. The bloody clashes reported in the Far North Province during late 1993 and early 1994, albeit difficult to track, may have included regime security sweeps against NUDP supporters, not just the official version's ethnic disputes, smuggling episodes, and bandit or army incursions from Chad.[83]

Violence subsided in 1993, but two obvious dangers remained and a third emerged. First, never to be discounted, if unlikely, the CPDM's isolation could precipitate a Beti gamble with a military coup to keep the regime in power. Second, a longer-term risk, regional constituency differences between the SDF and the NUDP -- South and North, Christian and Muslim -- ominously resembled those found in Nigeria. Third, the newly complicating factor was the militant Cameroon Anglophone Movement (CAM), rallying since 1990 to the veteran, often imprisoned dissenter, Albert Mukong, especially since its first All-Anglophone Conference gathered 5,000 people at Buea in April 1993.

This anglophone tangent may prove to be the most volatile factor of all, by undercutting the SDF's claims for unified leadership of the opposition, and ultimately of Cameroon itself. The party's 1992 national convention at Bamenda emphasised 'devolution of powers',[84] and 'decentralisation' was the rhetorical focus the following year at Bafoussam, where not once in his 1 7-page keynote speech did Fru Ndi use the word 'federalism'.[85] Yet this was the very lowest common denominator of CAM's more narrowly anglophone politics. Its moderates sought a return to 1961-72 federal governance. Its militants wanted to dissolve the 1961 union and secede in a new nation, 'Ambazonia', from what they provocatively termed, to make their alienation clear, 'la république du Cameroun', the pre-1961 state.

The dilemma was clear, forcing to the surface perhaps the most dangerous fault line of 'la crise/the crisis': for all the francophones attracted on national issues of polity and economy by the SDF and its charismatic leader, they now risked losing anglophones. According to Fru Ndi himself, 'francophones believe that federation is separation',[86] a perception that influences them for a variety of reasons. At one extreme are those with genuine concerns for 'la patrie', intensified by crises in Somalia and Rwanda, and at the other are those motivated by an intense dislike of anything English. All find themselves faced by such mundane but important questions as the surplus of francophones over anglophones employed on the other's side of the language border, many of whom could lose their positions in any deconstruction of the unitary state.

Fru Ndi sounded statesmanlike and populist at Bafoussam in 1993 when calling for 'political, constitutional and administrative decentralisation, based on the democratic election of governors and other officials, within the context of a pluralist state', with details to be worked out 'by the people thernselves'.[87] It later became clear that what the SDF had in mind was 'a government of transition run by a Council of State for two years, while a new constitution and electoral code are drawn up'.[88] But Fru Ndi's statements could equally be interpreted as committing him to as little as possible about the future of Cameroon, papering over opposition gaps, rather than declaring himself and risking a split in the Union for Change coalition which the SDF had fashioned across language and ethnicity lines for the 1992 presidential poll.

There was a risk of splitting the SDF itself. The anglophones in the South West Province and the party's predominantly North West leadership have been uncomfortable partners since the SDF began. Two major factors from the deeper past were at work: the coastal population's persistent resentment over hinterland labour migration to its plantations, and its substantial sympathy for Nigerian alignment rather than the Cameroonian choice which prevailed mainly on the strength of hinterland votes in 1961.[89]

These differences surfaced again during 1994. In January, a South West tour by the SDF Secretary-General, Siga Asanga, was argued in *pro* and *con* newspaper accounts. The party's *SDF Echo* recognised the tension, but rejected 'balkanisation' of anglophones and advocated a common polity for them in any future realignment of Cameroon.[90] A parallel but critical article in the *Cameroon Post* turned on Asanga for 'inflated political ambitions to take over the Republic of Cameroon', and consigned him to the farthest wilderness. He 'should be delegated to the Far North Province to go sing his dreams about his government' in (reverting now to the dismissive use of French) a 'grande' Cameroon to satisfy him and others in the SDF labelled as 'francophile'.[91]

The second All-Anglophone Conference, 29 April-2 May 1994, also revealed differences. As reported by *West Africa,* its Bamenda Proclamation, repeating charges against the regime, recounting failed efforts to enter into a 'dialogue' with Biya directly or (through France's embassy) indirectly, went far beyond SDF readings of the same evidence:

> The imposition of the unitary state on Anglophone Cameroon in 1972 was unconstitutional, illegal, and a breach of faith ... the minimum redress adequate to right the wrongs done [is] the restoration of the federal form of government ... [failing negotiation on this agenda, the newly established Anglophone Council should] thereupon, proclaim the revival of the independence and sovereignty of the Anglophone territory of the Southern Cameroons, and take all measures necessary to secure, defend and preserve the ... integrity of the said territory.[92]

The conference chairman, Ekontang Elad, a leader of the South West's Liberal Democratic Party (LDP), which stands outside the SDF's Union for Change, admitted, when interviewed, the danger that 'the multiplicity of Anglophone pressure groups' was eroding support for Fru Ndi, but was justified by the implacable hostility to anglophone leaders in Cameroon as presently framed.[93]

With SDF constitutional policy unsettled along the decentralisation-federalism axis, with separatism resurgent outside its ranks, disarray plagued many anglophones. As nothing else domestically could, this cushioned Biya's regime, which claimed the high ground of national unity -- indeed, even the rhetorical luxury of

140

invoking the Biafra spectre from parts of Nigeria contiguous with and historically linked to English-speaking Cameroon -- as well as charging anglophones with treachery.[94]

Cumulatively, therefore, in mid-1994, Cameroon faced political stalemate. CPDM recovery looked unlikely, and the local elections originally scheduled for 1993 had not yet been called. The opposition pointed out that CPDM appointees still controlled Cameroon's 279 rural and urban councils, rendering any vote meaningless, apart from enabling the regime to harvest the filing fees of all candidates.[95] The next national elections scheduled for 1997 offered no more obvious solace. With no civilian political scenario favouring the CPDM, the possibility of a military coup could not be discounted. But factors cited above also threatened the SDF at all levels: its national mobilisation against the regime, its direction of an opposition coalition, its own integrity. The NUDP appeared to be stagnant.

Are the major parties likely to negotiate (perhaps induced by foreign pressure), and if so, when? If the CPDM does not recover, and if the SDF and/or the NUDP cannot effectively replace the current regime -- in other words, if the so-called 'end game' is protracted -- Cameroon could by a further loss of central political ground become much more unstable and violent in the years ahead.

Prospects For Democratisation

What can be learnt about Cameroon from recent Africanist scholarship on state, civil society, and democratisation? For example, Robert Fatton has charted Senegal's comparable earlier story-- succession to a patriarch president, elite and popular dissent, and party pluralism -- so as to frame the same key operational issue which Cameroon's deeper crisis raises now: how will class choices within the elites be decided?[96] Having already emphasised the significance of the Cameroon map created by standard electoral and party politics since 1991, there is no question about the need for more micro-level studies throughout the country -- such as that, for example, by Kees Schilder for the Mayo Kani *département* in the Far North, which revealed the local impact of ethnicity, religion, chieftaincy, and patronage in the 1992 presidential ballot. [97] Such research would discern interest groups, determine elite alignments, link local and regional to national politics.

But it is doubtful whether such conventional forms of analysis based on vote counts and their local dynamic adequately measure Cameroon politics since 1990, especially in areas where larger, more transient and volatile populations than those studied by Schilder have built and sustained the resistance. In November 1991, for example, I watched 15,000 in Bamenda's football stadium challenge Fru Ndi for three hours and reverse a decision taken by the SDF executive that day to end 'villes mortes' (the strike continued until the year's end). There is surely a place for more open-textured analyses of Cameroon's lengthening and probably deepening crisis.

Domestic Factors

Fru Ndi is a case in point, whatever his original interests, actions, and intentions, and whether or not he can keep expanding his class, ethnic, and linguistic following. Mobilising Bamenda in 1990, scorning the Yaounde Declaration and taking personal risks to his safety in 1991 before he was well known abroad, his staying power

142

and steady rise in support against long odds confound conventional wisdom. Here is a riveting campaigner using Pidgin speech, Panama hats, and traditional Grassfield gowns in a popular idiom no other Cameroon leader remotely rivals. Fru Ndi verifies the place in current African politics of what James Manor calls the 'theatrical and imaginary' dimensions of populism,[98] and Michael Schatzberg finds in the working language, imagery, and metaphor of opposition to the state, often neglected by the 'narrowly exegetical Afro-Saxon tradition'.[99] They echo two important Cameroonian scholars who emphasise the connections between political structures and rhetoric in their critiques of the state, Achille Mbembe and Celestin Monga.[100] Fru Ndi could long ago have held high office had he bargained for it, or played politics conventionally all along, but those in the opposition who *did* so have receded and are despised by the many they alienate as much as admired by their static or falling number of supporters.

Like its charismatic leader, and despite its problems cited above, the SDF warrants more attention than it has received. There is not much detailed analysis available for parties which have framed Africa's opposition politics since 1989.[101] Few had any credible past (unlike the UPC, whose squandered legitimacy is a Cameroon tragedy). Many of the new creations took cynical advantage of tactics meant more to subvert than to support political pluralism (some in Cameroon were regime-financed, like the MDR), and most of those more legitimately based proved ephemeral. In franco phone Africa, parties were secondary to the *Conférence nationale* opposition strategy, often led by less overtly 'political' people from churches, the legal profession, and human rights groups, considered the appropriate forces to muster against 'monarchist' presidents.[102]

The SDF, however, represents anglophone Africa's arguably more diverse arena of multi-party politics, as in Botswana, or at least a more internally competitive single-party practice, as in Tanzania. Zambia, Kenya, and Nigeria are countries where political parties, though manipulated and beleaguered, have rallied post-1989 oppositional forces.[103] This is markedly the pattern among Cameroon's anglophones, identifying *sine qua non* their language and

143

the entire legacy of the pre-1972 British-based federal constitution, school system, civil service, and common law as a plundered minority's grievances against the unitary state. Not neglecting the national conference strategy, they are simultaneously developing the SDF as a working governance alternative and, as shown above, pushing into historically hostile francophone terrain despite trials or errors like the boycotts of schools in 1991, and (debatably) the legislative elections in 1992, and the anglophone stresses of 1993-4.

Local in origins, the SDF constituency and appeal are now significantly regional and diverse. The party has not yet achieved its real objective, national mobilisation, but it certainly transcends 'politicized ethnic sentiment', Samuel Decalo's justifiably dismissive terms for so much party development since 1989.[104] It likewise challenges Fatton's view of most of Africa's current opposition movements as essentially defensive, constraining and deceiving rather than shaping democratic or revolutionary forces, and of civil society's fractions as enclaves of 'survival' or 'hopeful resignation', seeking means of subaltern exit from 'the exploitative domain of a secular, predatory state'.[105]

Naomi Chazan's recent commentary may be the most appropriate for the SDF and Cameroon. She shares much of Decalo's and Fatton's scepticism, citing the salience of 'the heterogeneity of the social order rather than ... the coalescence of civil society', and the character of civil society's components as 'often inward-oriented, pointedly detached from the market and the state' instead of advancing public policy at the national level. She adds the warning that 'urban-based, essentially middle-class groups at the forefront of the recent protests have in the past been active in supporting authoritarian rule'.[106] These cautions do apply to the SDF and the regional business interests, teachers, church representatives, credit unions, and still more private finance channels it most clearly speaks and acts for; their commitment to the unemployed and truly dispossessed is not yet established.

But Chazan notes also the 'strong pluralist tradition' in former British Africa where, compared with francophone states, 'multiple

membership is commonplace and associational diversity more noticeable' in civil society. The SDF thus far justifies and reinforces her
placement of Cameroon's 'institutional arena' among Africa's more
promising settings for the 1990s.[107] It has policy papers now in place
covering the national spectrum of extra-constitutional issues. It has
weathered a leadership controversy (especially during 1993 between
Fru Ndi and Bernard Muna) without fragmenting. It has held
national congresses attended by hundreds in both anglophone
Bamenda and francophone Bafoussam. It has recruited senior regime
figures like Sengat Kuo (who joined Fru Ndi in 1992), and organised
the Union for Change alliance. It has established footholds within
public opinion abroad, where Fru Ndi's travels to Europe and
America resemble many earlier paths to African presidencies. There
is momentum and broad potential legitimacy in all this, *if* the SDF
can contain centrifugal constitutional forces between and within the
language communities.

How deep into Cameroon society do Fru Ndi and the SDF tap?
This is not yet clear. The use of Manor's and Schatzberg's
approaches, and more research like Richard Vengroff's for Mali,
beyond the public testimony of the leader and the party congresses,
into funding, membership rolls and sustained activity (not just street
rallies) in urban quarters, markets and farms, and among women,
would help and are under way.[108] Meanwhile, the best available
evidence is what happened in the core areas of the SDF preceding its
wide gains in the 1992 presidential poll. The general strike during the
latter half of 1991 has been discounted by those using conventional
indices, which tally its heavy economic cost to the estimated two
million people who were directly or indirectly involved, and make it
seem misguided. I prefer the view that the strike, in more relevant
terms, created the discipline of a non-violent resistance movement,
significantly reduced the state's revenue base, and stretched security
forces, whose units at times protected civilians in the opposition.
They were called on to punish, and even turned against each other.[109]
It gave Fru Ndi and the SDF a praxis and legitimacy to counter the
state's, and an experiential edge over all its rivals.

The party has not yet proved, in its internal structures, that it has the capacity to forge 'democratic experience' by Chazan's criteria- specific notions of authority, distributive justice, conflict resolution, and respect for the rule of law. [110] Nor does yet meet Michael Bratton and Nicholas van de Walle's broader criterion of 'an alternative ruling coalition with a sustainable multiclass social base and a coherent platform for governing' in place of discredited, exhausted regimes.[111] Only the test of holding power would prove or disprove such capacities. None the less, the SDF has the potential to advance Cameroon's associational life beyond the negative and zero-sum politics conjured up by Fatton's remarks about 'armies and *macoutes*' and 'narcocratic' regimes, when arguing that the state in Africa has moved from parasite to predator, and that ruling classes will continue to 'disarticulate' or co-opt elites and to subordinate masses engaged in recent protest politics in Africa.[112] The SDF looks more likely, if it ever takes or shares power, to relax than to reinforce the state's grip - - a prerequisite for gains in human rights, accountability, associational space, and service beyond its own constituencies, key indices for any definition of democracy.

Fatton and others may be correct about the fragile, suspect nature of so much African political opposition. But by mid-1994, the capacity of Cameroonians to starve the state was as striking as the regime's capacity to punish the people, and the presumed powers of incumbency looked more like burdens. On one basic measure, the state's extractive capacity, van de Walle reported that revenue collected in 1991 was only 15 per cent of the previous year's level.[113] Hence the possibility that Cameroon's regime is 'soft' enough to be dislodged, by negotiations or by elections, and with minimal casualties, before it can subvert the opposition or destroy it by force. And such a scenario may be quietly brokered beyond the borders, where international conditions since 1989 favour regime autocracy less than previously.

External Pressures

Consider France's role as 'la crise' developed. For example, Biya's speech in October 1991, rejecting (again) a national conference and calling for elections, resembled very closely the script that Michel Aurillac, a veteran African policy official, had published five days earlier in the *Cameroon Tribune.*[114] Only France gave enough foreign aid for Cameroon to meet IMF and other debt schedules, to pay key military and civilian personnel, and to keep the state's official budget expenditure constant since 1989-90. But we have seen Cameroon's autocracy falter, even with this support, raising doubts about France's 'cost-benefit' calculations for its presence there.

Similar questions have emerged in other French client-states. In the neighbouring Central African Republic, when the August 1993 presidential elections were annulled, France cut off aid which had kept afloat a less-than-essential client, thereby forcing General Andre Kolingba to capitulate and accept electoral defeat.[115] In Gabon, after the President for a quarter of a century, Omar Bongo, had been pressed to the polls in December 1993, his announced majority of 51 per cent brought bloody street protests and charges of French collusion in chicanery. Almost concurrently in the Congo, dozens were reported killed in clashes between the regime headed by Pascal Lissouba and the oppositiori.[116]

Outside the French orbit, civilian politics generated unhappy parallels in Cameroon's most substantial neighbour during 1993, when Moshood Abiola's regional political base became a successful pan- Nigerian opposition movement, only to have its electoral victory annulled. General strikes broke out in Lagos and at petroleum refineries and ports, followed by international sanctions. This Nigerian *démarche* demonstrated the challenge that pluralism has mounted against autocracy there, revived at very high risk in mid-1994 by Abiola's renewed claim to the Presidency, his jailing on treason charges and resumed strikes.

Indeed, Nigeria's better-known situation and France's interests there became an instructive vantage point for the geo-political tangle

147

of Cameroon's domestic and foreign experience early in 1994.[117] Sovereignty in the remote Bakassi Peninsula area of the fishing, trading, and now petroleum coastal border of Nigeria and Cameroon has been ambiguous for a century. A skirmish in January 1994 left Nigerian soldiers on ground where Cameroonians were effective residents/ occupiers, and France sent a modest complement of troops and equipment in accordance with the terms of its defence pact. But a week later France and francophone Africa jointly announced a 50 per cent devaluation of the CFA currency, the half-century base of fiscal security and *coopération* at the heart of French sub-Saharan strategy.

Obviously it is necessary for all the client states of France to assess the changing situation very carefully, especially Cameroon, for Nigeria, now rivals Côte d'Ivoire as France's biggest African market. It is also, through Elf-Aquitaine, France's largest crude oil source, and a business site for 130 more French companies. Disorder on the border between Nigeria and Cameroon no longer automatically privileges the latter in France's policy. As explained by *Jeune Afrique*, 'si les intérêts diplomatiques français sont à Yaounde, les intérêts économiques sont à Lagos'.[118] Then, additionally, President Franois Mitterrand became in July 1994 the first foreign head of state to visit Nelson Mandela's South Africa in a working rather than a ceremonial capacity. The salience of both Nigeria and now Southern Africa alongside the weakened franc zone in French sub-Saharan strategy looks obvious, just as the CFA devaluation marks an ever larger priority of Europe over Africa for France. No more so, one must assume, than to President Biya, confronting a Fru Ndi now perhaps less menacing to France as an anglophone or Nigerian 'fifth-columnist' threat.

France in fact supplied debt relief and another fiscal transfusion which Cameroon parlayed into a new $115 million IMF credit in March 1994, but these are less than ever reliable, more than ever isolated channels, especially if Biya keeps refusing to agree to a political transition. Ministerial shuffles, such as removing the most powerful and vilified Beti politician, Joseph Owona, from direction

148

of the office of the presidency in July 1994 did nothing to reduce the creditability gap. Cameroon's economy is in foreign receivership, with the French cushion deflated. Its politics could soon also be determined largely abroad, on grounds favouring the opposition over a regime with a poor bargaining position.

The evolution of the presence of the United States during the 1990s suggests how Cameroon may fare, exposed to post-cold war international realities as French cover recedes. Evidence emerged of an American initiative challenging French strategic dominance, which openly distressed the CPDM regime. Without judging what directed the balance of Washington's motives, obviously based on a complex mix of interests and altruism -- oil, Douala as an industrial free zone (IFZ), human rights, democratisation -- note the contrast between early 1991, when American support was Biya's to count on, and late 1993, when governmental aid levels dropped by half and the US Agency for International Development suspended its operations.

The US Ambassador to Togo moved to Cameroon in 1992, bringing her experience of a rough confrontation between a notorious regime and a determined opposition. The former Assistant Secretary of State for Africa, Herman Cohen (who cancelled a mid-1991 visit while in office to show disapproval of regime reprisals), spoke in Douala in mid-1993 about Cameroon's need for decentralised governance and a national conference,[119] very much against Biya's unitary state legacy from France. Cameroon operates in no vacuum; unyielding regime politics are unlikely to be tolerated indefinitely, and the blockage of the stalemate could be dislodged by the pressure of outside interests.[120]

Outlook

Cameroon's experience since 1990 drives the wedge against African autocracy deeper. It is premature to call it democratisation as long as further opportunism and repression remain real or potential scenarios. As for the future, Cameroon's uncertainties are highlighted by two simultaneous versions of its reality in the immediate wake of

IMF funding renewals in March 1994. In President Biya's broadcast to his compatriots, 'The international finance community's attitude clearly shows the confidence it places in our country'.[121] By way of contrast, for *Le Monde* the same day, francophone Africa was:

> une situation quotidienne douloureuse. Exemple caricatural, celui du Cameroun fantômatique--le gouvernement ne se réunit pratiquement plus-- éprouve le plus grand mal à payer ses fonctionnaires ... a situation routinely painful. A caricature example, ghostly Cameroon - the Government hardly meets any longer - experiences the greatest hardship paying its civil servants ...[122]

The sense here was, once again, of political forces juxtaposed but adrift, hardly recognisable from the other's perspective.

But neither text located Cameroon on the firmer ground, despite many reservations, that *I* believe it now claims among African nations where the populace, to quote Richard Sklar, constitutes a 'national workshop [which] contributes to the aggregate of democratic knowledge and practice' and, to use Jean-François Bayart's similar eloquence, works to 'invent democracy' autonomously.[123] Africanists and democratic forces need to watch Cameroon's immediate future more closely than they have its recent past.

End Notes

[71] Mark W. DeLancey, *Cameroon: dependence and independence* (Boulder and London, 1989), surveys the background; Nantang Jua, 'Cameroon: jump-starting an economic crisis', in *Africa Insight* (Pretoria), 21, 3,1991, pp. 162-70, dissects the economy of the late 1980s; and Nicolas van de Walle extends that analysis into the 1990s, especially in 'Neopatrimonialism and Democracy in Africa, with an Illustration from Cameroon', in Jennifer A. Widner (ed.), *Economic Change and Political Liberalization in Sub-Saharan Africa* (Baltimore and London, 1994), p. 129-57.

[72] Van de Walle, loc. cit. p. 138. This process reduced the number and narrowed the base of some 1,000 leaders earlier identified as 'la Classe dirigeante' in Pierre Flambeau Ngayap, *Cameroun: qui gouverne? De Ahidjo à Biya, l'héritage et l'enjeu* (Paris, 1983), pp. 8ff.

[73] Cited in *Cameroon Post* (Limbe), 30 May 1991.

[74] How quickly and far this unrest spread can be gauged from a critical editorial in *Le Messager*, 18 July 1991, attacking Biya: 'let him and his western supporters know that what is now happening in Cameroon is a popular revolt which the *opposition* is trying hard to contain'. My translation.

[75] These details are from my Bamenda period of residence, with crowd estimates much below opposition claims. See *Amnesty International Report*, 1992 (London, 1992), pp. 79-81, for the situation country-wide.

[76] *Cameroon Post*, 27 September 1991, covered this episode, confirming the accounts of my Bamenda informants.

[77] For a typical reaction in the critical press about Biya's evasion of reforms, see the heading and editorial in *Le Progrès* (Douala), 14

January 1992, entitled 'Trahison de la tripartite: la constitution confisquée'.

[78] *Cameroon Tribune*, 11 March 1992.

[79] See National Democratic Institute for International Affairs, *An Assessment of the October 11, 1992 Election in Cameroon* (Washington, DC, 1993), Executive Summary and Appendix XI.

[80] Published in the *Cameroon Tribune*, 23 October 1992, and reproduced in ibid.

[81] See interview by Fru Ndi in *Africa Report* (New York), March-April 1993, p. 63.

[82] As in November 1993, when Fru Ndi sought refuge in the Dutch embassy after the SDF had been prevented from holding a press conference in Yaounde.

[83] *The Herald* (Douala), late January 1994, *SDF Echo* (Yaounde), 28 February-9 March 1994, and *Jeune Afrique* (Paris), 14-20 April 1994 .

[84] 'Proceedings of the First National Convention of the Social Democratic Front, May 21-26, Bamenda 1992', p. 29.

[85] Official SDF documentation with its seal, including Fru Ndi's keynote Bafoussam speech and cognate material, August 1993.·Reports in *West Africa* (London) conveyed a firmer sense of federalism as SDF policy than primary sources justified; vexing constitutional issues were being skirted more than resolved in party circles.

[86] *West Africa*, 7-13 March 1994, p. 388.

[87] Fru Ndi's keynote Bafoussam speech, August 1993.

[88] *West Africa*, 7-13 March 1994, p. 388.

[89] The revival of anglophone politics was anticipated in DeLancey, 1989, op. cit. The tensions between the South West and North West Provinces are documented in Peter Geschiere and Piet Konings (eds.), *Proceedings of the Conference on the Political Economy of Cameroon -- Historical Perspectives / Colloque sur l'économie politique du Cameroun -- perspectives historiques* (Leiden, 1989), Parts 1-2. Two electoral features have differentiated coast and hinterland, albeit 31 years apart. In 1961, 96,000 of the 136,000 vote margin for Cameroon over Nigeria in British Southern Cameroons came from Bamenda's six electoral districts. In 1992, during the presidential poll, Fru Ndi won 86 per cent of votes in the North West as against 52 per cent in the South West. The evidence is complex. Many anglophones now work in both the SDF and CAM; Mukong was an honoured guest at the SDF Bamenda convention in 1992.

[90] *SDF Echo,* 28 February -9 March 1994.

[91] *Cameroon Post,* International edition, 24 February-3 March 1994.

[92] *West Africa,* 20-26 June 1994, p. 1090.

[93] Ibid. p. 1091.

[94] As long ago as 1991 the regime alleged that the senior anglophone army officer, General James Tataw, was plotting against it on Nigeria's behalf.

[95] 25 *Le Messager,* 27 January 1994.

[96] See Robert Fatton, Jr., *The Making of a Liberal Democracy: Senegal's passive revolution, 1975-1985* (Boulder and London, 1987). According to the Carter Center's 'Quality of Democracy Index', Cameroon was termed 'ambiguous' in its commitment to democratic transition, behind 32 other African nations, alongside (among others) Zaïre, in mid-1991 at the peak of tension. By mid-1993, following the elections, Cameroon had moved up a revised scale to the status of a 'directed democracy', as had Kenya, but behind 15 polities deemed to

153

be 'democratic'. *Africa Demos* (Atlanta), 2, 1, 1991, p. 11, and 3, 2, 1993, p. 19.

[97] Kees Schilder, 'La Démocratie aux champs: les présidentielles d'octobre 1992 au Nord- Cameroun', in *Politique africaine* (Paris), 50, 1993, pp. 115-22.

[98] James Manor (ed.), *Rethinking Third World Politics* (London, 1991), p. 4.

[99] Michael G. Schatzberg, 'Power, Legitimacy and "Democratisation" in Africa", in *Africa* (London), 63, 4, 1993, p. 445, introducing a valuable study, couched in vernacular idioms, which argues that indigenous cultural measures of political *legitimacy* are preconditions for, and more important than, any forms of democracy as understood elsewhere.

[100] Achille Mbembe, 'Pouvoir des morts et langage des vivants: les errances de la mémoire nationaliste au Cameroun', in *Politique africaine,* 22, 1986, pp. 37-72, and Célestin Monga, 'La Récornposition du marché politique au Cameroun (1991-1992)', Groupe d'études et de recherches sur la démocratie et le développernent économique et social, Douala, 1992. For a profile of this non-governmental organisation since its origin in 1990, see Honoré Guie, 'Organizing Africa's Democrats', in *Journal of Democracy* (Washington, DC), 4,2, April 1993, pp. 119-23.

[101] Richard Vengroff, 'Governance and the Transition to Democracy: political parties and the party system in Mali', in *The Journal of Modern African Studies* (Cambridge), 31, 4, December 1993, pp. 541-62, offers a micro-analysis with wide range and predictive features, but the parallel is limited by the demise of Mali's regime-party in 1991 and the survival of Cameroon's thus far.

[102] See John R. Heilbrunn, 'Social Origins of National Conferences in Benin and Togo', in ibid. 31, 2, June 1993, pp. 277-99; Jacques Nzouankeu, 'The Role of the National Conference in the Transition to Democracy in Africa: the cases of Benin and Mali', in *Issue: a*

journal of opinion (Los Angeles), 21, 1-2, 1993, pp. 44-50; and the on-going work of Pearl Robinson.

[103] See, for example, Githu Muigai, 'Kenya's Opposition and the Crisis of Governance', in *Issue,* 21, 1-2, 1993, pp. 26-34, for Cameroon's closest parallel.

[104] Samuel Decalo, 'The Process, Prospects and Constraints of Democratization in Africa', in *African Affairs* (London), 91, 362, January 1992, p. 31.

[105] Robert Fatton, Jr., *Predatory Rule: state and civil society in Africa* (Boulder and London, 1992), pp. 60 and 77.

[106] Naomi Chazan, 'Africa's Democratic Challenge', in *World Policy Journal* (New York), 9, 2, 1992, pp. 287 and 303. Patrick Chabal, *Power in Africa: an essay in political interpretation* (New York, 1992) in key ways echoes Chazan for Cameroon and Africa at large.

[107] Chazan, loc. cit. p. 291. Note also Dwayne Woods, 'Civil Society in Europe and Africa: limiting state power through a public sphere', in *African Studies Review* (Los Angeles), 35, 2, 1992, pp. 88-91 and 97, for similarly more hopeful soundings on African civil society which Cameroon (though not cited) reinforces.

[108] Women in markets and street stalls, for instance, enforced Bamenda's 1991 general strike in those sites; their massed groups swelled the demonstrations, and one particular association warned off strike breakers and taunted and obstructed the military in open defiance (perhaps as an example of women's public sanctions identified in a growing local literature by the term '*anlu*').

[109] Bamenda-based police warned civilians against gendarme sweeps in 1991, when Radio France Internationale also reported gunfire between local and national security forces in the vicinity of Foumban.

[110] Chazan, loc. cit. p. 289.

[111] Michael Bratton and Nicolas van de Walle, 'Popular Protests and Political Reform in Africa', in *Comparative Politics* (New York), 24, 6, 1992, p. 440. As for Cameroon, 'Elites almost invariably prefer the status quo to the unknown" Ibid. p. 434.

[112] Fatton, *Predatory Rule,* p. 86, in a section headed 'Exit and Anarchy: the descent into hell'. His scholarship on morbidity in the African state is given Cameroon specificity by Achille Mbembe, 'Provisional Notes on the Postcolony" in *Africa* (Manchester), 62, 1, 1992, pp. 3-37. Only slightly less bleak is the 'escape' and 'exile' language in Rene Lemarchand, 'Uncivil States and Civil Societies: how illusion became reality', in *The Journal of Modern African Studies,* 30, 2, June 1992, p. 187.

[113] van de Walle, loc. cit., p. 146, using *Africa Confidential* (London) as source. If this was anywhere near the truth in 1991, no substantial recovery since then can have occurred. Incidentally, Cameroon's football achievements in the World Cup during 1994 offered the regime few of the redeeming populist features that characterised 1990.

[114] *Cameroon Tribune,* 6 October 1991.

[115] *Le Monde* (Paris), 31 August 1993.

[116] Ibid. 5-15 December 1993.

[117] This paragraph and the next two condense a host of materials briefly, and try to make provisional sense for Cameroon of issues that cannot be discussed at length or judged with certitude here, especially CFA devaluation and the impact on anglophone politics of what is surveyed. Key sources, often mutually at odds, include a series of financial analyses in *West Africa,* October 1993-January 1994; *Le Monde,* 13-20 January 1994; unclassified documents of US Departments of Commerce and State, February and March 1994; *Jeune Afrique* periodically, but especially 19-25 May 1994; *Cameroon Post* and *The Herald,* as well as other domestic opposition newspapers.

[118] *Jeune Afrique,* 19-25 May 1994.

[119] *West Africa*, 9-15 August 1993, p. 1408.

[120] For a revealing current of informed, cautious, influential opinion in the United States, see *Africa Demos*, 3, 2, 1993, p. 17: 'Unless Cameroon's political forces can be brought together to arrive at a comprehensive agreement about the country's future, the current political and economic drift in the nation is likely to provoke violent social conflict'. Cameroon is specified as 'an ideal test case' for 'preventive diplomacy'.

[121] This translated text of Biya's speech on 23 March 1994 is from the *US Foreign Broadcast Information Service, Africa* (Washington, DC), 24 March 1994.

[122] *Le Monde*, 23 March 1994.

[123] The passages are from seminal essays of the early and mid-1980s. Richard Sklar anticipated democratic reconstruction in his 1982 speech 'Democracy in Africa', reprinted in Sklar and C. S. Whitaker, *African Politics and Problems in Development* (Boulder and London, 1991), p. 260. Jean- François Bayart, 'Civil Society in Africa', in Patrick Chabal (ed.), *Political Domination in Africa: reflections on the limits of power* (Cambridge, 1986), p. 124, drew more cautiously on events then placing regimes in question.

The 1994 paper developed further, during my 1995 and 1999 returns to Cameroon, into the introduction and the first two and last three chapters of a book co-authored with Joseph Takougang, *African State and Society in the 1990s: Cameroon's Political Crossroads* (Westview Press, 1998). It also framed my own 2008 Langaa Press book, *Cameroon's Social Democratic Front: Its History & Prospects as an Opposition Political Party* (1990-2011).

These three writings on politics touched on the promises and the limits of recent Cameroonian affairs. They followed lines of inquiry and judgment that scholars will recognize particularly in the Africa-wide work of Bayart and Richard Sklar (my principal mentors in this field, through their writings, like July and Bjornson earlier). They contained predictive features that prove to be, at best, only partly justified at the time of this book's publication. As the Epilogue amplifies below, my aspirational reach did not fully satisfy the analytical needs of the scholarly tasks at hand. Except for the truly prescient among us, such is the path and fate of the historians of recent and contemporary Cameroon whose ranks I've joined.

Epilogue

A quarter century's perspective

My shortest Cameroon writing is the most visceral, and appropriately concludes this volume.

A third research trip, 1995, gave me the opportunity to complete the *Abbia* text and to move forward with research and writing on politics. Three deaths that year, Prince Dika Akwa's, the priest-scholar Father Engelbert Mveng's by savage murder in circumstances never seriously investigated by Cameroonian authorities, but especially Thomas Melone's, fused many elements of my scholarship, and my dispositions and judgments regarding Cameroon.

As noted in Chapter 2 above, Melone was Fonlon's peer and counterpart, prominent with *Abbia* and both versatile and prolific as a university scholar and teacher before less talented, more favored conformists within the Biya state apparatus superseded them as public intellectuals. With Fonlon dead since 1986, it struck me that Melone's passing in 1995 (even though his last twenty years were increasingly erratic and marginal) signaled a productive Cameroon cycle's end, with both now gone. This left, until his own death in 2001, Mongo Beti as the lone surviving, openly defiant figure from that generation in my study's cultural and political arenas. Returned from thirty years of "absence" in France (perhaps he was an "exile" but I've learned to use that word with care, only when I'm certain a person so classified uses or prefers it, which doesn't apply here), Beti was in 1995 harassed at his Yaounde bookstore and assaulted when he publicly displayed his scorn for Biya at a presidential motorcade (his 1997 SDF Mbalmayo legislative candidacy would be neutralized by CPDM money and invalidated by an electoral commission ruling).

Only a few younger people's combination of imaginative range, intellectual autonomy and critically engaged but not necessarily party-linked politics, like Pius Njawe's at home and Ambroise Kom's

159

among others who took up lives mostly abroad (although Kom returned home in 2012, to l'Université des Montagnes), maintained such front line critiques of public life in Cameroon through the 1990s. When invited by Abiola Irele to write a Melone obituary, it therefore seemed timely to review and reflect on my original culture-education-language-development study, now enlarged by politics. The result was the *Research in African Literatures* 29, 1 (1998), pp. 197-198 text, reprinted below.

The television coverage of Melone's August 1995 memorial service significantly influenced this "IN MEMORIAM" writng. The state's representative at the funeral was Joseph Owona, perhaps the most despised of Biya's deputies in his multiple cabinet ministries and the office of the presidency among the Cameroonian dissidents I have met over many years. Will I stir memories among readers here, who were also CRTV viewers then, by retaining to this day the sense that Melone's family, with Owona in their midst that day, were appalled by the indignity of his presence? I trust I did not then, or now, err by conflating what seemed their outrage and my own dismay about what was happening in Cameroon at the time. With the regime imprinted on the Melone family's grief in 1995 and on the country at large, in the wake of and despite the 1990-1992 challenges, this episode disclosed the array of forces and perhaps the suspension, even the eclipse of hopeful prospects after years of risky challenges to obdurate authority within and across the interlocked domains of knowledge, imagination and power I was studying in Cameroon. This Melone obituary was meant to convey my sense of the country's condition by the mid- and later 1990s.

In Memoriam
Thomas Melone

Three deaths within ten weeks in 1995 claimed pioneers among Cameroon's formidable generation of men of letters, arts, and human sciences born between the wars. Father Engelbert Mveng was savagely murdered in April, in circumstances governments unlike Paul Biya's would have judicially probed but his has not. Thomas Melone and Prince Dika Akwa passed more "peacefully" at mid-year. Like their works however, their travails in exile and prison link them with Mveng, and turn this appreciation of Melone not just to his accomplishments but also to the sad truths which turn visionaries who should be honored in the Africa they served so well into discards, and worse, at the hands of their own country's rulers, who so lack their victims' virtue(s).

Melone in many ways defined the buoyant culture of Cameroon's first independent decade, as scholar, teacher, and one of African literature's foremost tribunes anywhere. A prototypical African student-nationalist in *Présence Africaine* and La Fédération des Etudiants d'Afrique Noire en France circles during the 1950s, the common enough distinction of expulsion from France in 1961 was no bar to his appointment as the first Cameroonian on the faculty of the new national university. Its indigenization process provided chances Melone seized, mastering the terrain where his own talents and state patronage converged. The talent showed in a variety of publications leading to books on Mongo Beti, Chinua Achebe, and Camara Laye in the years (1972-74) before his eclipse. As for the patronage, how can one top the story Ambroise Kom recounted (in "Une autre victime de l'ogre," a 3 July 1995 *Le Messager* tribute using what Kom believed to be Melone's last scholarly interview, 1991) of Melone hosting an occasion with Léopold Senghor as speaker and Ahmadu Ahidjo as guest in the university's Amphi 300?

Surely Melone's finest achievement, however, was to turn that talent and patronage to the advantage of African literatures in a

161

Yaounde setting where its creators, scholars, teachers, and students flourished, perhaps as nowhere else in Africa. As head of a Department of African Literature framed to all genres and to comparative study, he encouraged, edited, introduced, and saw to press a wealth of other peoples' works alongside his own. *Mélanges Africaines* (1973) best displayed the venture's promise and flair. Based on a Yaounde colloquium introduced by Senghor, dedicated to the Senghor-Ahidjo friendship, praising the latter for the cultural policy underpinning his own efforts, this product of Melone's passion used a mask-music-motion ensemble in vibrant colors on the front cover and the indigenous script by Cameroon's Sultan Njoya on the back. Nearly 400 pages of text covered oral narratives, offered critical perspectives on twentieth-century writers ranging from Africa's giants (Senghor, Kane, Soyinka) to its newer voices (Grace Ogot, most strikingly), and engaged the diaspora as well (Hughes, Ellison, Césaire, a Washington-DuBois retrospective). The last pages reproduced in Senghor's own hand the manuscript of his elegy for Martin Luther King, Jr. *Mélanges* visually and verbally celebrated, in words Melone's preface used to state his own cultural bearings, "L'originalité criarde de l'apport négro-africaine a la civilisation de l'Universel" 'the clamorous originality of the Negro-African contribution to the Civilization of the Universal.'

His orientation was challenged, as Marcien Towa and others opposed both Melone's negritude scholarship and his proximity to Ahidjo state- craft while autocracy grew. But Melone was a critic as well. A 1966 essay in Abbia, Cameroon's ranking journal of culture, about "les dangers du fonctionnarisme" in the university anticipated more broadly the aid and deference intellectuals gave the regimes which so deformed Cameroon's public life in the next three decades. There were sharper episodes--Richard Bjornson cited a protest about university pay to the French surpassing what Cameroonians received for the same work. In any event, the program he built faltered and Melone's career collapsed after 1974, leading to unhappy French exile while Ahidjo still ruled, and then village solitude as a fish-pond farmer during his later years. Melone sat in the National Assembly for

Biya's party from 1988, then (a last defiance?) as a UPC deputy from 1992. But both he and this party of his youth had lost vigor, and his sporadic press interviews vented fretfully against lesser men in lesser times than his own. Perhaps Melone took consolation as Douala people served and boasted of tilapia from his ponds, but his old age was marginal. No one watching CRTV cover his funeral will forget that cruel sight: a brutally combative Biya cabinet loyalist, Joseph Owona, representing the state, a family clearly offended by his presence.

A comparison of Melone with the anglophone Bernard Fonlon is intriguing. Both were early seminarians whose mature years in the same program and humanist style were globally recognized, and whose links to those in high power were complex, equivocal, and worth study for what they tell of how knowledge and power in Cameroon intersect, and of its language communities' scholarly elites. "What might have been … " had they, their peers, those they taught, not encountered such a security-driven, careerist cast of mind and narrowed clientelism in those who still rule Cameroon, and those who serve them? What began to flower on Yaounde's campus (and elsewhere in Africa) is scattered, significantly off-shore in Columbus, Bayreuth, and other points of the academic compass. Many who did follow Melone's and Fonlon's leads in Cameroon later chose ever more dependent paths of preferment, academic prebends, to the detriment of letters and its autonomy, joining the state apparatus and imposing its panegyric cult on the legacy of their elders and (one must say) betters. Now they face Mongo Beti, Ambroise Kom, and others who seek to restore that legacy, for a contest between the regime's "organic intellectuals" and these critics now informs Cameroonian culture, parallel to the challenges in Cameroon's politics.

Thomas Melone perhaps rests more hopefully now in spirit than in the last years of a troubled but at times inspirational and wonderfully productive life in African letters.

I devoted the rest of my 1995 research and all of 1999's, during my (thus far) final time in Cameroon, to assembling political evidence, primarily about the SDF. Coverage (as direct observer) of principally its Bamenda base of operations but also in other settings at intervals between 1991 and 1999, including its 1995 Maroua and 1999 Yaounde national conventions, and (thereafter, from abroad) its presence and experience since 2000, were the touchstones for this research. The 1998 and 2008 books cited above were its products.

How does Cameroon register from my perspective, nearly fifteen years since my last sojourn there but while I remain engaged with the country's people and prospects a quarter century since my first arrival? The story of oppositional energy in the early 1990s has given way to the inertial burden of regime incumbency. My 2008 book recounted the SDF's origins and (then) current condition, and speculated about what lay ahead for it, and Cameroon, in ways that now appear to have been overly optimistic.

However Cameroon's future experience plays out, two sharply contrasting views about the decade my writings primarily covered, the 1990s, will likely dominate and contest its story, with a third reading in the wings that I associate with Achille Mbembe and those of his persuasion, conceding the Cameroon state less direct command and general influence over its citizens (or, more correctly, in this view and my own, its <u>subjects</u>), many more of whom have denied its legitimacy and "exited" its domains, some with impunity and even profit, than just the insurgents of 1990-1992. One of the two more conventional views favors the *status quo*, arguing that the 1990s "movement" politics of opposition to the state was misguided (thus, a 1991 sovereign national conference was truly <u>not</u> for Cameroon), and that the presidency's, CPDM's and security force's firm grasp saved a centrifugally pulled nation from the chaos that overtook neighbors near and far. It cites Cameroon's relative stability and peace compared with "what might have been worse." The alternative view in my writings, aligned with most others I know of, looked beyond such a low common denominator, toward Fonlon, not Fame Ndongo. Crediting the cultural and political opposition as a positive force within Cameroon and potentially for Africa at large, I and others argued that governance by "le pouvoir" suppressed the wider community's knowledge and imagination, especially their most progressive sources, and failed to develop the country's abundant natural and human resources toward "what could have been better."

But I overestimated civil society's cohesion and its capacity to discipline the state, and also the SDF's vanguard momentum; a measure of their diminished standing at ten year intervals, 1990, 2000,

165

2010, makes the latter point. My knowledge of the Cameroon state's routines was insufficient to gauge how its excesses could be addressed and curbed, and my primary focus on its critics' thoughts, actions and affiliations, which interested me far more, as "movement politics," than the state's agents and workings, missed some salient marks. The ultimate practical and scholarly reckoning about the story of culture and politics told in this volume--how will the history it conveys fit the larger historiography?--will remain fluid until at least the contours and outcome of the presidential succession to Biya become known. As of 2013, if less than prescient as an historian of recent and contemporary Cameroon, I have brought attention to those who have generated hopeful cultural and political visions for Cameroon's and Africa's futures in the four texts reprinted here and in the two later books that completed my sequence of political publications. I would be pleased if this volume prompts a Cameroonian's fuller investigation of issues and problems my writings leave unresolved.

My concluding thoughts are twofold. First, perhaps quixotically, are there room and a good reason for the book linking Cameroon and Canada I thought of writing but never will? Connections like their common official bilingualism sketched early in this text remain pertinent in history and for current and future purposes, with MacLennan and Benjamin among the guides. The countries share complex histories and problems, like their constitutions, as well as long borders with powerful, prideful neighbors, so that Canadian experience is a potential reference point for Cameroonians. Both are members of the Commonwealth and la Francophonie, international networks with notably different histories, styles and practices that could be mutually instructive across the "North-South" spectrum. Canada's Guelph and Laval universities have historical connections to Cameroon that the latter's counterparts might cultivate, bringing people and projects together through bilateral or broader working linkages like the Canadian International Development Agency's. Deceased Cameroonians like Fonlon, Ela and Albert Ndongmo had Canadian experience and there is at least one significant "Canadian in

Cameroon" parallel, Cardinal Paul-Emile Léger. What they and others have done could provide guidance ahead. These are historical and contemporary leads a book could investigate to practical and reciprocal advantage, good will as well as common interests permitting

Finally, and more realistically, there <u>are</u> room and a good reason for a Cameroonian to write the country's intellectual history that Mongo Beti called for in Ambroise Kom's *Mongo Beti Parle* (2002), and also to relate it to Cameroonian culture(s). It should expand Chapter 2 here, examining the diverse intersections of knowledge, imagination and power, incorporating all persuasions, and adding people I omitted or merely sketched who (within or beyond my culture-education-language-development point of entry) have influenced and contested Cameroon's public realm, with consequences for statecraft. François Sengat Kuo exemplifies the possibilities and nuances, if pursued beyond this book's brief paragraph about him as a student nationalist while in France, a poet of distinction, a mainstay in the Ahidjo and Biya presidencies and (if what I've often heard is true) the latter's lead writer for *Communal Liberalism*, then (in quite a reversal, just before his death) a major consultant to the oppositional coalition during the early 1990s. Adding to many already named above, in Chapter 2 or elsewhere, Henriette Ekwe, Ndiva Kofele-Kale, Célestin Monga and Simon Munzu are among "public intellectuals" whose careers (even if many were taken abroad) have salience for the public realm and merit attention. And why not dramatists, and Lapiro and other musicians, whose productions and voices have contributed significantly to "word of mouth/radio trattoir" channels of opinion through cassettes, CDs and independent radio, so that popular culture confronts "le pouvoir" in ways with often higher stakes and risks than in more formal written channels? However aligned to individuals, issues and expressive mediums, the book should update and expand Bjornson's pioneering text and in particular his synoptic Chapter 14, "Cultural Politics in an Age of Transition," which anticipated but did not incorporate "la crise/the crisis" of the early

167

1990s (a sadly premature death in 1992 denied Bjornson that further study).

Three features would especially help such a book. First: more attention than Bjornson gave to anglophones, whose collective presence is now greater than during his time, and thereby also to Cameroon's version of MacLennan's two Canadian solitudes. Second (what's so elusive, and a reason to promote Cameroonian authorship): while avoiding essentialism and recognizing nuance when "identity" is at issue, a sharper delineation of Cameroon's ethnic features in both customary and partisan senses, and their cleavages, especially for that <u>most</u> elusive and problematic constellation of forces, the "Bamileke factor." Third: beyond what either Bjornson's or my own work offer in their textually literal fashion, the incorporation of more experiential, imaginative, metaphoric probes of state and civil society, along Mbembe's and others' more contemporary lines, especially broad gauge anthropological writings like Peter Geschiere's and region-specific studies like Jean-Pierre Warnier's on the Grassfields and Piet Konings' from Douala westwards, which neither conceptually nor factually impose the nation state as a defining construct on Cameroonians' experiences. Without denying the state's and its institutional framework's salience, they cross or collapse political boundaries and more thoroughly address important cultural, economic and social domains like age, ethnicity, gender, income, occupation and religion. They focus on, and tease out, practices that both reinforce and challenge the state, including its local operations and operatives.

Such coverage would, collectively, amplify Francis Nyamnjoh's and his colleagues' writings since the late 1990s on "the politics of belonging" and even Tadadjeu's work: what is intrinsic and what is instrumental about language and community for Fe'efe'e, Bafut and Mundani, and who does or does not benefit from efforts to promote them? Consider in this regard a passage (already cited above) from the "bilingualist" Fonlon's "Education through Literature" (1977) about his mother tongue that, despite how the early part of this book

168

contrasts him with the "multilinguist" Tadadjeu, actually bridges them: "I do not worship English. I worship Lamnso." An intellectual history thus framed, with cultural dynamics significantly included, would articulate both integrative and disintegrative features of (quoting Bjornson's sub-title) "the National Experience," a domain for study that I believe remains intact and pertinent but needs sharper delineation to capture its *longue durée* twists and turns and the impact of the past quarter-century's tumult.

Should, or do, foreigners' writings on recent culture and history have any influence on what happens in Cameroon? If so, it's my closing hope that the texts from the 1990s gathered here, and the current text connecting them, will alert their Cameroonian readers to what Richard Sklar, in a phrase cited earlier, now repeated here, once called the "workshop of democracy" potential for Africa at large, and that they will both recognize part of their own narrative in this book and find it suggestive about and applicable to their current and future experience.

www.ingramcontent.com/pod-product-compliance
Lightning Source LLC
Chambersburg PA
CBHW022319280326
41932CB00010B/1153